No Labels
No Limits
You don't need a diagnosis to dream

Melissa Gorrie

Published by Change Empire Books

www.changeempire.com

All rights reserved

Printed on demand in Australia, United States and United Kingdom

Edited & formatted by Change Empire Books.

Book cover design by IvanovITCH

Photography by Wendy Taylor

This book is sold subject to the condition that it shall not, by way of trade or otherwise, be lent, resold, hired out, or otherwise circulated without the publisher's prior consent in any form of binding or cover other than that in which it is published and without a similar condition including this condition being imposed on the subsequent purchaser.

The scanning, uploading, and distribution of this book via the internet or via any other means without the permission of the publisher is illegal and punishable by law. Please purchase only authorised electronic editions and do not participate in or encourage electronic piracy of copyrightable materials. Your support of the authors' rights is appreciated.

While the authors have made every effort to provide accurate internet addresses at the time of publication, neither the publisher nor the authors assume any responsibility for errors or for changes that occur after publication. Furthermore, the publisher does not have any control over and does not assume any responsibility for author or third-party websites or their content.

EBOOK ISBN: 978-0-6487453-7-2

PRINT ISBN: 978-0-6487453-8-9

Welcome to Holland

Welcome To Holland by Emily Perl Kingsley

Copyright©1987 by Emily Perl Kingsley.

All rights reserved.

Reprinted by permission of the author.

I am often asked to describe the experience of raising a child with a disability - to try to help people who have not shared that unique experience to understand it, to imagine how it would feel. It's like this......

When you're going to have a baby, it's like planning a fabulous vacation trip - to Italy. You buy a bunch of guide books and make your wonderful plans. The Coliseum. The Michelangelo David. The gondolas in Venice. You may learn some handy phrases in Italian. It's all very exciting.

After months of eager anticipation, the day finally arrives. You pack your bags and off you go. Several hours later, the plane lands. The flight attendant comes in and says, "Welcome to Holland."

"Holland?!?" you say. "What do you mean Holland?? I signed up for Italy! I'm supposed to be in Italy. All my life I've dreamed of going to Italy."

But there's been a change in the flight plan. They've landed in Holland and there you must stay.

The important thing is that they haven't taken you to a horrible, disgusting, filthy place, full of pestilence, famine and disease. It's just a different place.

So you must go out and buy new guide books. And you must learn a whole new language. And you will meet a whole new group of people you would never have met.

It's just a different place. It's slower-paced than Italy, less flashy than Italy. But after you've been there for a while and you catch your breath, you look around.... and you begin to notice that Holland has windmills....and Holland has tulips. Holland even has Rembrandts.

But everyone you know is busy coming and going from Italy... and they're all bragging about what a wonderful time they had there. And for the rest of your life, you will say "Yes, that's where I was supposed to go. That's what I had planned."

And the pain of that will never, ever, ever, ever go away... because the loss of that dream is a very very significant loss.

But... if you spend your life mourning the fact that you didn't get to Italy, you may never be free to enjoy the very special, the very lovely things ... about Holland.

Chapter 1

She wasn't breathing.

My previous baby had come into the world screaming, so I knew straight away that something was wrong. Looking at the doctor and nurses, I could see that they were thinking the same thing.

"Let's get this little one some oxygen," the obstetrician said, wiping his brow with his forearm.

They raced her to the small trolley on the other side of the room.

My heart was so heavy it felt as though it were sinking into my chest as everything hit me.

Was my baby alive?

"Is it going to be okay?" I asked my husband, who was holding my hand and looking paler than I had ever seen him.

"I don't know," he replied.

I really wanted him to lie to me and tell me that my baby would be fine, just to reassure me. Nothing in that moment was reassuring me. I wanted to get up off the bed and go over to see for myself, but I couldn't move.

One of the nurses stayed with me, but the doctors and other nurses were with my baby, all of their attention occupied with bringing it back.

"Will my baby be okay?" I asked the nurse. Fat tears started to roll down my cheeks.

"Waaaahhhhhh…"

A cry came from the other side of the room: my baby was crying and breathing. It was the best sound I had ever heard and brought so much relief. I took a huge breath, feeling like I had forgotten to breathe the entire time I was waiting for the baby's cry – and we were taking that first life-giving breath together.

The nurse smiled at me as the tears ran down my cheeks. That was the reassurance I needed.

"Is my baby a boy or a girl?" I asked her.

"Don't you know?" she said, a little surprised that I hadn't found out during the pregnancy.

I shook my head. "I wanted it to be a surprise."

"You have a beautiful baby girl," the doctor said. " You can hold her very soon."

It seemed like forever before they brought her to me. While I waited, I stared at the bright light they had her under, but I couldn't see my little girl.

"She is beautiful," my husband said as he went over to her. "She has so much hair."

They wrapped her up and brought her to me. She had a full head of thick black hair and was just perfect.

I held her close and kissed her head repeatedly, tears streaming down my face. As she continued to cry, I felt both relieved and overwhelmed.

Welcome to the world, Lauren Emma Carey. What an entrance she had made.

Since she had passed all of their tests, Lauren didn't have to go into a humidicrib, and after a few days they were happy for us to take her home. I was relieved to finally be able to take her home. She was healthy, and after the huge ordeal I had been through, I was just grateful it was all over.

I was glad to be home from the hospital. I had missed Rebecca, who was 17 months old. Although she had enjoyed staying with her Nanna and Pop, she was also very excited to be home with her family and her new baby sister. All Rebecca wanted to do was hold Lauren and watch her every move. I knew how she felt; I loved having Lauren safely at home and just kept watching her, taking in every moment of our little family, now grown by one.

The first night we brought Lauren home, she only woke once all night. She slept so well that I bragged to everyone that I had the perfect child.

Unfortunately, my perfect baby didn't sleep like that again, and I felt that I might have been too quick to tell people how wonderful she was.

But even with her always waking during the night, she had ten perfect fingers and ten perfect toes.

That's all that matters, isn't it?

Chapter 2

Two months later, alone in the house with both my little girls, things began to get worse rather than better. Lauren started having problems feeding and refused to drink.

I would sing to her to try to calm her, swaying while standing and rocking while sitting, but nothing seemed to work.

I really wanted to breastfeed Lauren because I wanted things to be as natural as possible; I really enjoyed that bonding time, not to mention how good it was for her health. I had had no trouble feeding Bec, so I couldn't understand why this time was so hard.

Had I forgotten how to do it properly? Was something I had eaten disagreeing with my baby?

I didn't have any answers. When I tried to feed Lauren, she would start off okay but then become agitated and cry very quickly. I tried to do exactly what they had gone through at the hospital about how to get her to latch on, but she didn't want to and would just pull her head away.

"Come on, Lauren, you must be hungry," I'd say to her. "This will help you to grow up to be big and strong."

I tried again and again, but she just kept refusing. It seemed the harder I tried, the more she refused.

"Why?" I wondered. "Why don't you want to drink? What am I doing wrong?"

I was not giving up; I knew that eventually she would have to drink. She couldn't keep going like this.

Maybe she was just being stubborn.

"Now, you have to drink! I am not going to keep doing this with you!" I was becoming more frustrated and unsure of myself. "Please, Lauren! Please, you have to drink or you will get sick."

But even though I tried every way I knew, she still wouldn't drink. I would give up and break down in tears because I wasn't being the mother that I wanted to be for my little girl. I couldn't work out what I was doing wrong, but it was becoming a real concern.

I needed help, and a friend suggested that I talk to the health nurse about Lauren's feeding. When I arrived at the health clinic, the nurse was really lovely and listened to my concerns. I tried feeding Lauren while I was there so she could go through what I was doing wrong, step by step. We tried different ways of getting Lauren to latch on and settling her while she was feeding. I tried wrapping her up tight so I could have more control of her tiny body since she seemed so determined to move away from me.

Unfortunately none of these suggestions seemed to work. The nurse did suggest trying to bottle feed her, but I really didn't want to give up on breastfeeding. But I realised I might not have a choice. We couldn't continue like this, and I had to do the best thing for Lauren.

I gave in and agreed to try giving her a bottle. I went out and bought the formula and the bottles and the steriliser that went in the microwave and then went home, sterilised it and gave her a bottle. But she didn't drink it like I thought she would.

This was supposed to be my solution. Why wasn't she drinking from the bottle? What had I done wrong now?

Nothing had changed. Lauren continued to cry and refused to drink. Unable to get the help I needed, I tried reading books to find the answers. I asked friends for their advice and even went to the doctor to get help. We tried every different type of formula.

"She might be lactose intolerant," I was told.

"My daughter settled when I tried these types of teats." I tried every type of teat, with no success.

"Try thickening the formula." The small amount she drank just made her constipated.

Lauren was also a very spewy baby and would throw up after most feeds, if she actually drank some. It was less like a bit of wind and more like projectile vomiting. I would sit Lauren on my knee after getting her to drink, and she would vomit like in horror movies, to at least a metre from where we were sitting. It was hard to believe that such a little girl could do that. I soon learnt that whenever we went out, I not only had to take Lauren a spare set of clothes or three, but also to put in a spare shirt for me.

While trying to get help with Lauren's feeding problems, we visited the doctor so regularly the receptionists recognised my voice when I called. They would put us straight out the back when we got there and give Rebecca toys to keep her busy. They were so kind; they could see I was struggling and would often look after Rebecca while I talked with the doctor.

As the weeks went on, Lauren's crying turned into screaming, and I knew that something more had to be done. There were days where I would show up at the doctor's office with tears running down my face because I couldn't hold them in any longer. I despaired of finding answers for how to get Lauren to drink without screaming.

My family lived about eight hours away, and the few friends that I had soon stopped coming around. It was so difficult to have a conversation when your screaming child needs to be consoled.

My husband spent more and more hours at work; I'm sure he didn't want to deal with his screaming daughter and upset wife. Not that I really blame him for not wanting to be there – I would probably have done the same, given the option. But I couldn't do that to Lauren, and I most certainly couldn't do that to Bec.

"Please come home," I would beg him. "I really need your help."

There was always an excuse for why he had to work late or start early. I was left home all day on my own to deal with the Lauren situation, which slowly became worse as each day passed.

"What are you doing?" I asked one morning, still half asleep. I'd been up with Lauren and hadn't long been in bed. "It's still dark."

"I'm going to work," he told me. "I didn't get a job finished last night, so I need to get it done this morning before the customer picks it up."

I had heard these excuses so many times before.

"Do you think you could come home for lunch?" I said. "I can make you a sandwich."

"I will see how I go," he said, getting out of bed. "Go back to sleep."

I knew that meant he wouldn't be coming home for lunch. Again.

In addition to my husband's absence, I was worried about Bec, who was missing out on so much just because she was Lauren's sister. I couldn't take her to the park to play or join mother's groups so she could make friends. The few times I tried, I ended up leaving early because I couldn't control Lauren's crying. I felt so guilty for taking Bec away from the fun activities other kids got to enjoy.

I was failing her as a mother.

I was failing my friends.

I was failing my husband

I was failing myself.

I had never felt more alone.

Yet I loved the sanctuary of my home, where the neighbours knew why there was screaming coming from my house. Our house wasn't the best house on the street, but I loved it. It was a brick house that wasn't too old; it had very plain colours, and I added my own touches with a few pieces of timber furniture that Dad had made. I had restored a cupboard to make a TV cabinet and actually used the doors from that to make a collage with our wedding photos. The curtains I had made helped to decorate the rooms, and I had put extra effort into making the girls' rooms special for them.

I was happy to hide at home, escaping from people's judging eyes when I took the girls out and Lauren would cry and then start screaming.

When I did have to take the girls out, I dreaded it. I was always worried that Lauren would become upset.

"She's hungry," people would say.

"She needs a cuddle."

It didn't take long before I grew tired of trying to explain our situation to strangers and began to just nod and smile as we moved on.

My in-laws quite often took Bec back to their place, which wasn't far away. I was grateful she not only got to spend time with them and her cousins but also had time away from her screaming sister and crying mum.

I really tried not to cry in front of Bec, waiting until I had a shower to let it all out. Often, I just sat on the shower floor and bawled my eyes out. I was so lost and sad, and I just didn't know how I was going to keep going.

How will I make it through the next hour?

Why me?

I hated feeling like this, but sitting on the bathroom floor, I had to let some of that emotion out in the form of tears. It was a way to release some of the pain I was feeling, and then I would emerge from the bathroom with red, swollen eyes, ready for the next onslaught of mayhem. Even though I had just been in the water, it always felt like all of the tears had drained the moisture from my body. Some days, the pressure would be too much. No matter who was around me, I couldn't hold it in any longer and just couldn't stop the tears.

I tried to spend as much time with Bec as I could, playing games and reading to her. She loved it when I read her books, and I really cherished that time together. Sometimes I made up stories for her.

"Once upon a time, there was a beautiful princess called Bec who lived in a huge castle," I would tell her. "One day, she had a little sister who was very noisy, but Bec didn't mind; she loved her sister very much and helped look after her. Bec would ride on her horse to a magical garden and pick beautiful flowers." She would look up at me and smile, and I would continue telling her the fairy tale about wonderful Princess Bec's life.

I would lay beside her in bed and read to her, running my hands through her curly red hair, and often she would fall asleep. Bec learnt to sleep through Lauren's screaming as a necessity. If it kept her awake as well, I would have had two very tired little girls as well as a sleepy mum.

Often, I put Lauren in her cot, shut the door, and just let her cry, so that I could spend some time with Bec.

Because we lived on a large block, my only solitude was at our back boundary. I would walk down there as Lauren's screams grew quieter, and just stand there, imagining I was somewhere else completely, maybe on a deserted island or a cruise boat sailing the oceans.

I just wanted one minute in which I didn't have to hear that screaming. Just one minute.

I wondered what I had done in my life to deserve such a cruel punishment.

I didn't know how much longer I could do this.

Sometimes, I stood in the doorway to Lauren's room and just looked at her as she screamed her little lungs out. She seemed so normal other than the screaming. She was such a beautiful baby. Her hair was still thick and black; she hadn't lost any of it. Her skin was so smooth and flawless. Her crazy little crossed eyes were such an unusual colour.

How could she be so perfect in every other way?

Why won't she stop screaming?

There were times I thought that if I just put a pillow over Lauren's head to quiet her, just for a minute...

I didn't want to hurt her; I just needed her to stop screaming for a moment. Just a little moment of silence.

Please. I just need a few seconds.

As I took slow steps into her room, the screaming seemed to get louder.

Please, Lauren, you need to stop.

As I stood beside Lauren's bed, I reached out and bundled her into my arms.

I am so sorry.

I would never hurt you.

I love you so much.

I held her close to me and kissed her head, and then stood there for a few minutes, just hugging her little body, while she continued to howl. I knew she was screaming because she was in pain. What else can I do?

It was horrible having these thoughts, but I needed help. I knew that I couldn't do it to her. I loved Lauren. I really did; I couldn't not love my child. But the thought was there – not to end her life at all but just to have that little moment of silence I so badly craved. I knew I had reached the lowest moment in my life, and I couldn't see a way out of the situation.

Chapter 3

"Your child isn't normal," the neurologist told us, as though he were telling us about the weather. My whole body just froze in that moment. I didn't believe the words that came out of his mouth about my beautiful daughter.

How could he make that diagnosis? How could she not be normal?

My mind was racing, but in that second, my heart broke into a million pieces.

Only a few days earlier, I'd been excited that I was finally going to get the help I so badly needed. After enduring so much with Lauren in her first three months of life, I was grateful that I would finally be getting some help from an expert.

Our doctor sent us to Brisbane to a sleeping and eating clinic for babies. I was so relieved that someone was going to help me. Bec went to stay with my in-laws, and Lauren and I packed our bags for the week-long stay.

While there, they went through Lauren's feeding technique and we tried several different ways of giving her a bottle, but it really didn't make any difference. She continued to get upset and refused to drink. We also tried different ways to get Lauren to sleep, wrapping her tight so she felt secure, among other things, but again had no success. I was starting to wonder if I was ever going to overcome these problems.

I would sit there in this little room, looking at my beautiful little girl; with her thick black hair and beautiful olive skin, she looked so perfect. Her lips were a rosy pink, like she was wearing lipgloss. Her eyes were crossed, but they were the most magical eyes I had ever seen: green with a golden tinge. I wondered how well she could see with eyes like that, but that really that was the least of her problems.

When Lauren was awake, she always moved her arms and legs. That's how I knew when she was asleep, because she was still – and quiet, of course. I assumed she was just active and didn't think too much of it. But while we were at the clinic, one of the nurses said that one of the doctors was coming to see us about Lauren, as they thought the movements that Lauren made needed investigation at the Royal Children's Hospital.

At the time I was at the clinic on my own again; this was something that I was getting used to by this stage, but I told my husband that he needed to be here for the appointment at the children's hospital. So he picked us up, and we went and saw a neurologist.

Sitting in that waiting room, I had so many thoughts running through my head. What if there is something wrong with Lauren? I desperately hoped they could give her something to help with the screaming, that we could all go home and live happily ever after.

As I sat there, holding my baby and looking around at all of the other parents and kids, I was taken aback by the kids in wheelchairs and kids with tubes in their noses. I wondered how they could sit there playing with smiles on their faces. It must have been so hard, being one of those parents. And I had to wonder: how many times had they come to this hospital?

I couldn't help but think. The whole situation made me question why we were sitting there. There were so many kids in this huge waiting room who needed help more than we did. Surely we shouldn't be wasting these specialists' time, not when Lauren moving her arms and legs was really no big deal. The other parents and kids are the ones who need help, not us.

But we were there anyway, and it seemed like hours before they finally called Lauren's name.

We went into the consulting room, where the neurologist and several trainee doctors looked at Lauren for a really long time. They performed some simple tests to check reflexes and how she reacted to them moving her. When they asked questions about my pregnancy and her birth, I gave them the condensed version: "The pregnancy was easy, with no complications. I went into labour three times for hours until the contractions were just a minute apart and then they just stopped and we were sent home. On the third time, about ten days after the first contractions, the doctors broke my waters. Lauren had the cord around her neck and wasn't breathing when she was born. They quickly revived her; she passed all her tests and didn't have to go into a humidicrib."

I was very factual, as I just wanted to explain briefly what had happened so they could get on to divulging their great knowledge and start to provide answers.

"After about eight weeks," I went on, "she started having trouble feeding and would cry a lot. Things progressively got worse, and now she screams a lot and won't drink very much, which is why we're at the clinic."

They proceeded to ask questions about Lauren's movements, as if everything I had just told them was irrelevant to what they wanted to know.

"When did you notice that she had these involuntary movements?" he asked.

"I'm really not sure," I said. "She's been doing it for a while, but they've been getting progressively more noticeable. I was more concerned about her feeding and trying to keep her from crying." I was trying to justify why I hadn't been overly worried about these movements. "What do you think it is?"

That was when he announced that my child wasn't normal.

"The movements that Lauren makes aren't normal," he said, "and they need further investigation." He proceeded to explain that they were going to do tests, to see if they could figure out what the problem was, and that they would contact us with the results.

We left with more questions than answers. I was so confused about what had just happened. And as if the whole experience hadn't been enough to make me want to fall in a heap on the floor and cry my eyes out, we also had to do a blood test on the way out of the hospital.

It was so horrible holding her tiny little arm while she was screaming in pain. Three others tried to hold her still while one of the nurses attempted to draw enough blood to do the tests they wanted. I held her tight just so they could do the test quickly and the nightmare would end. The doctors had to find something in her blood that would solve the problem, because I never wanted to go through this again. Walking out of the hospital, I was emotionally drained, as though someone had just sucked all of the life right out of me.

As we started driving back to the clinic, I just broke down. How could someone just come right out and tell you that your child isn't normal? It wasn't what I wanted to hear.

Not my baby.

Surely this couldn't be happening to me!

I was in complete shock. It felt like someone had taken a piece of my heart, like my world was spinning out of control. Once we arrived back at the clinic, my mind was whirling so fast, with so many thoughts, that I couldn't catch any of them.

The other mums at the clinic were so supportive and held me, which was just what I needed. My husband came back to the clinic with me and stayed for a few hours until I calmed down. He did offer to stay but I didn't want him to. I needed time to process this on my own. So he drove the two hours home.

All I wanted to do was hold Lauren and make her better. But somehow I knew I couldn't. All of us were at the clinic to get help with our babies' feeding or sleeping difficulties. With Lauren, we were there for both.

She wouldn't drink from a bottle properly and she wouldn't sleep. The one thing she could do was scream. It wasn't just a cry for attention, or because she was hungry – she was screaming in pain as though someone was trying to cut her arm off. She screamed not only while trying to drink but also most of the day and night. I was exhausted, and this was to be my last resort for finding solutions to fix my daughter.

As it turned out, this was just the start: I was about to embark on an extremely hard journey.

Chapter 4

How is that you wake up to find you no longer have the same life and the same future – that there is an uncertain feeling about what is about to come?

We went home after our week at the clinic and tried to get back into some kind of normal behaviour or, at least, our new kind of normal. I couldn't get those doctor's words out of my head. "Your child isn't normal." It was like it was on a constant loop, and as hard as I tried, the words wouldn't go away.

We stayed in touch with the neurologists at the Royal Children's Hospital, but nothing showed up in any of the test results.

I was so disappointed.

I wanted there to be an easy fix.

I wanted answers and a quick cure.

The specialists were deciding what to do next – maybe an MRI or more blood tests. Both worried me, but we had to wait. Lauren's sleeping and eating were getting worse, which I hadn't thought was possible.

My world was a mess.

My house was a mess.

I was a mess.

Getting to do normal things like brushing my hair and teeth was a luxury. There was always a basket full of washing to be done, overflowing on to the floor. Wet clothes were still sitting in the washing machine from the day before that just hadn't got hung out. And there were dirty dishes in the sink.

I did try my best to at least have dinner cooked when my husband came home from work, because that's what good wives do. Growing up, my mum was a stay-at-home mum and always made sure that she had a hot dinner for Dad when he came home from work. It seemed like that should be an easy thing to accomplish, but some days it wasn't. I tried to maintain a clean house and to keep on top of the chores, but there weren't enough hours in the day.

I was exhausted beyond belief. Lauren wasn't sleeping at all. The doctor had given me several different types of medications to help her sleep, but I felt like such a bad mother for forcing the medication into her throat and holding her nose so she would swallow. It was the only way I could get her to take it – and most of the time, half of it wasn't taken and was instead sprayed all over me.

After all the struggle of giving her the medication, it still took over an hour to start working, and even then she only slept for 20 or 30 minutes. Don't get me wrong – I was grateful for those minutes of silence and a quick catch-up on some sleep, but it was such a vicious cycle. So many people told me that the medication and doses we were giving our baby should be enough to make her sleep for hours; I could only hope that one day that might come true.

At the time, I could only focus on one minute to the next, on just putting one foot in front of the other to make it through each day. It was the hardest thing I have ever had to endure, and I had never felt so alone.

Through all of it, the thing that probably kept me sane was having Rebecca. She was a beautiful little girl, with fiery red hair and a temper to match. She made me smile when I didn't think I could, and I knew that I had to hold it together for her.

Rebecca was an adventurous girl. She started walking when she was nine months old, and it didn't take her long to start running. Even though we had an enclosed area outside for her to play in which was taller than she was, she'd climb it, straddle the top rail, and throw herself over, escaping to play with the kids next door. They would quite often bring her home, and I was so busy with Lauren that I often didn't even notice that she was missing. Rebecca would climb everything and always had scrapes and bruises from accidentally falling. She ran around constantly and once tripped on a mat, fell into the shower and ended up with a huge black eye.

I felt really sorry for Bec. She didn't choose to have a sister who was so demanding, and I didn't want her to miss out on life. It was so hard trying to give her a normal life; I didn't even know what 'normal' was supposed to look like anymore.

By the time Lauren was getting down to drinking less than 20ml a day, I had reached the end of my rope. It didn't matter what I tried; I couldn't get her to drink. I completely lost it at a regular doctor's visit and told him I didn't know how I was going to keep on doing this. We had an appointment with the reflux specialist at the Royal Children's Hospital in a few weeks, as they suspected that that was causing her pain, but it seemed so far away. But after many trips to the doctor, he told me I couldn't get in any earlier.

I was getting desperate, so a few days later we drove the two hours to the emergency room at the Royal Children's Hospital in Brisbane. After explaining the many difficulties we were having with Lauren, they suggested we try and give her a bottle so they could see what she did. So I did; I was only too happy to show them exactly what I had been dealing with.

I sat there giving her a bottle, expecting her to refuse it and start screaming. But this time she didn't. This time she drank the whole thing, without one cry.

This can't be happening. Why would you do this?

I was devastated.

I hadn't been able to get her to drink in days, and yet here she was being a perfect child. We were there to show the doctors what was normal for us, and this certainly wasn't it. And so they suggested that I take her home and come back for her appointment to see the specialists.

I think I was in shock, but I just fell apart and started to cry. "You can't send us home," I sobbed. "This isn't normal. I can't do this anymore. I don't think I will survive if I have to do this any longer."

Thankfully, he could see that I was obviously having a meltdown and decided to admit her and kept her for further observation. Maybe it was me they were observing, but by that point, I didn't care. I was so grateful for his decision, because I knew in my heart that I wouldn't make it until her appointment without any help.

Lauren did eventually show her true colours when she drank other bottles in the hospital, with her screams making it clear that something was wrong. So they started to do more tests to see what was going on. We got to see the specialist almost two weeks early. They decided that we should come back in a week and do a test where they would run a tube down her nose to her stomach and monitor her reflux for 24 hours.

Lauren, my husband, and I all went back to Brisbane for the test, which we were hoping would be the key to the answers we longed for.

It was absolute hell. They had to splint her arms so she didn't pull the tube out.

We stayed in Brisbane while they did the test, in a motel near the hospital. We went out to a large shopping centre to get some food, with Lauren in a baby seat on the front of the shopping trolley. I couldn't believe the number of people who stared at Lauren. The braver ones came up and offered us all sympathy. It was awful, and because she was crying a lot, more people's attention was drawn. I wanted nothing more than to hide my baby from the world and the judgement of other people.

To be honest, before all of this happened, I'm sure I would have stared at someone in the same situation. But on the other side, it was heart-wrenching having so many people instantly judge not only my daughter but also me as her mother. I was already struggling with my new life; having people examine us during an already difficult time was unbearable. So we went back to the solitude of the hotel room.

Lauren was awake and screaming for most of the night, and I honestly felt so sorry for the people who were staying in the hotel. It didn't matter what I did; nothing would console her. I must have walked up and down that room for most of the night, rocking and singing, trying to get her to sleep just a little.

I was so grateful to go back to the hospital after the 24 hours were up. It had felt like the longest day of my life. And, finally, we got some answers. The results showed that Lauren had severe reflux and was a borderline case for having it operated on. I was actually relieved to know the cause of most of her feeding difficulties and her screaming.

After trying many different medications and attempts to get the right dose, her reflux finally settled. We were able to reduce the acid that was coming up and lessen the frequency of her vomiting after she drank. It was such a relief that we eventually were able to help Lauren. Although she still had symptoms, she was crying and screaming less. And, more importantly, she was feeding again. She had lost some weight while not drinking, so we hoped that we could turn that around and nourish her body again.

Lauren was eventually on such a high dose of medication that the man who lived next door was taking the same dose as my four-month-old daughter. But it seemed to help, and I was so grateful to finally be able to give my little girl some relief from her pain.

The neurologist at the Royal Children's Hospital continued to perform tests to try to find out why Lauran was constantly and involuntarily moving her arms and legs. It seemed to get more noticeable the older she got. She had CT scans, x-rays, blood tests, MRIs, for most of which she had to be admitted to hospital and have a general anesthetic.

The hardest thing as a mother was taking her in for blood tests. I had to hold her down with someone else's help while the person taking the blood tried to find a good vein. Lauren would scream the place down and try to get away from the pain in her arm. They wouldn't normally get the amount of blood that they needed, but it would be enough to do most of the tests.

As a mum, I just wanted to find the solution to my baby's problem. There had to be an answer and an easy fix; we just had to figure out what that was. Every time we did more tests, I would go home and Google what the doctors were testing for. I spent hours looking at symptoms and comparing them to Lauren. I learnt that there were a lot of different syndromes out there, and spent most of my time thinking that the test had to come back positive, because she had all of the symptoms, and there was a cure which would fix her. Only to be disappointed when we went back to get the results and they didn't show us anything.

I finally decided that I couldn't continue to give myself this false hope. It wasn't that I didn't want to find a diagnosis for Lauren; I really did, so we could fix her, but I had to stop obsessing over every condition that the doctors looked into, as it was breaking my heart.

Just when I didn't think I could endure any more challenges, Lauren kept them coming. She started to do this thing where it was like she would get a fright, throw her arms in the air, and space out for a second or two before starting to scream. At first, I thought she was just sensitive to noises around her, that it was just a fright thing – but like most things with Lauren, it wasn't that simple.

This became more and more common, and every time she did it, Lauren would scream for an hour or more after. Even my many attempts to settle her really didn't make any difference. I must have sung "You Are My Sunshine" a million times to her; on the odd occasion, it seemed to help her settle.

There were times when it seemed like her screaming would never end, so I would take her to the emergency at the hospital. We would sit there for another hour, with her screaming, until we saw someone. I would go over her symptoms from when she was born to the present; I had that story down pat by now from telling it to so many doctors and specialists. Lots of waiting and checking files inevitably resulted in doctors who didn't have a clue what was going on; they always resorted to giving her antibiotics, in case it was an infection somewhere.

There were times when I'd drive to the hospital, talking to Lauren as she screamed in the back.

"I wish you could just tell me what's going on. Is it worth doing this drive to the hospital at 11 at night? Will they even be able to find anything this time? Please, Lauren, stop crying. I'm trying to do my best, but I don't know how to help you."

We'd finally get to the hospital and go through everything yet again with the girl at the front desk before taking our number and waiting with all of the other people. I always felt sorry for them having to listen to Lauren scream. I had no way of knowing why they were all sitting there in the middle of the night, but Lauren screaming at the top of her lungs couldn't have helped.

One particular night, I had attempted to give Lauren pain relief a few hours earlier, although I wasn't sure whether she had actually swallowed any of it. Maybe it was starting to work, or maybe she was just exhausted, but she eventually went to sleep. At that point, I figured there was no reason to see a doctor when I'd got the outcome I was after, and I definitely didn't want them to wake her up, so we left and I drove home for a few hours of sleep.

I know how the emergency room works with prioritising patients, but I could never understand why we always had to wait so long to see a doctor. My little girl was obviously in pain, and something wasn't right. I knew it wasn't the reflux again, as we finally had that under control. Now she only screamed like this after having one of her jump episodes. There had to be a reason for it.

I'd be at home, trying to console Lauren and questioning whether I should take her to the hospital. What if she never settles and something really bad happens to her? What if I am just overreacting? What if they think it is nothing?

They haven't helped in the past, so why would it be any different this time? Surely I am wasting my time driving up there when they won't do anything!

But what if they do find something?

Am I a bad mother if I don't take her?

Am I a bad mother if I do take her?

Please, Lauren, just stop crying. Please.

I was so torn as to the right thing to do. There were times when I made the decision to take her to the hospital, and there were times when I would just keep struggling at home.

Most of Lauren's first year was spent crying and being rocked. I really think the rocking was to help me, because it didn't make any difference to her. The specialist we saw thought she might be having seizures and tried to do an EEG. It used to blow me away that Lauren would do her jump thing at least three times a day – until we put wires on her head and hooked her up to a machine to monitor her brain activity, at which point she didn't do it at all.

In the first few hours of the EEG, we just hung around waiting, but nothing happened. I decided that since she would occasionally do it if there was a loud noise, I would 'accidentally' start dropping and banging things. But there was still nothing.

"Please, Lauren," I would beg her, "you need to show them so we can fix this."

Yet after being there all day with Lauren acting normal, we once again left with no answers.

The doctors did decide that even though she hadn't done it on the day of the test, there was a good chance she was having epileptic seizures. Since I didn't know much about seizures, it was described to me as like Lauren had a storm in her brain, with lightning and thunder, and they believed that was why she would scream after it.

Once again, we tried a lot of different medications and doses in an attempt to get them under control; eventually it seemed to help a little, but they never stopped. Every time it looked like the medication was working, Lauren's system seemed to get used to it and it started being less effective. We'd increase the dose and start the whole cycle again.

During her first year of life, Lauren had more tests done than it was possible to count. She had squint repairs done to her eyes as she had been born cross-eyed, which after everything else was a simple procedure. Even though she was medicated for her diagnosis of reflux and epilepsy, she still continued to have symptoms. She was also very constipated, and I had to give her enemas and suppositories and all kinds of different medications.

I don't really know how I survived that first year. Probably through necessity.

It was honestly the loneliest I had ever felt.

Even though I had Bec to keep me sane, I felt so abandoned by my husband. When he was home, we fought a lot, mostly about why he was always at work. I couldn't get him to see why I needed him there to help. I knew that he was struggling with Lauren – but so was I. He wouldn't talk to Lauren like he had talked to Bec when she was a baby. I don't think he really knew how to be around his problem child. If I'm honest, I really didn't like being around my husband then, and it was hard to remember why I married him in the first place.

Chapter 5

Don't do it! my heart had screamed at me.

You can't disappoint all these people, my head had replied, especially your dad and mum...

I had stood there at the end of the makeshift aisle, holding my dad's hand and looking at my family and friends; they were all so happy to be celebrating this special day with us. My soon-to-be husband stood at the far end of the aisle, smiling and waiting for me to start my journey towards him.

But my body was frozen. My stomach churned and I felt like I couldn't breathe.

"Are you okay?" Dad had asked, holding my hand a little tighter.

I don't know if I can do this. I don't know if I want to do this.

"Yes," I replied. I couldn't disappoint him again.

I had already been through a previous relationship my family hadn't approved of. Now I had a man who would take care of me, who my family liked, who ticked all of the boxes – except for the one in my heart. I did love him; I loved the idea of getting married, of buying our own house and having our own little family. I wanted the fairytale, every corny bit of it. I wanted the perfect marriage that my parents had, and my sister had, and my friends had.

I had pushed all the doubt in my heart back where it belonged, buried where I couldn't find it, and took that first step. As I did, I assured myself that it's okay to have a bit of fear. Everyone does.

But even the universe had been giving me signs I didn't want to listen to. On our wedding day, I was supposed to arrive at our outdoor ceremony in a helicopter. I wanted it to be spectacular – like a fairytale. That morning, though, it was pouring rain, and the helicopter wasn't an option. The manager at the resort where we got married, arranged to borrow a friend's boat to take myself, my dad, and my sister, who was my bridesmaid, to the waterfront reception. On our way to the reception, the boat started pouring out smoke.

My sister commented, "It isn't good when boats have smoke. There's a lot of fuel on board."

The smoke was overpowering and made us cough. We survived the short boat ride, but we all ended up having terrible sore throats. The smoke fumes were awful, and we later found out it had been caused by bad fuel.

When we arrived and escaped the smoke, we discovered that most of the guests were waiting for us inside, out of the rain, and so didn't even see our grand arrival.

Yet I walked down that aisle with a smile on my face, looked my husband in the eyes, and said "I do."

Looking back, there had been signs for a long time that this wouldn't be the perfect marriage.

We had decided that on my 21st birthday we were going to get engaged. We had even picked out the ring; he just had to pick it up, to give it to me as my present. I was so excited. That morning, he said that he still had to go pick up the ring but would do it later.

I had so many phone calls from friends and family throughout the day to wish me a happy birthday because we lived eight hours away from them all; I felt very loved but very alone at the same time. We lived with my boyfriend's parents next to the workshop where he worked with his dad and brother, so I kept checking as the day went on to see if he'd gone to get the ring.

When he came up to the house for lunch, I reminded him. "You still have to get the ring, remember?"

"Yeh, I know," he said. "I just have to finish these couple of jobs, to get them out, and then I'll go and get it." He smiled reassuringly at me. "Don't worry, I won't forget."

He was in that workshop all day. The day dragged on, until it was after 5pm and the jewellers was closed. And I knew he hadn't gone out to pick up the ring.

I was devastated. I sat in my room and cried and cried. He finally came in at about 7pm and found me.

"I'm sorry," he said, "I was just joking. I picked up the ring yesterday." He said it like it didn't matter, like I shouldn't have made such a big deal out of the situation. "I have the ring, here. Will you still marry me?"

How could he do that to someone he loved? Where is the romance?

Just joking? He couldn't be serious.

I certainly wasn't laughing. I was angry, sad, and annoyed. I couldn't understand why he would do such a thing to me. How could I marry someone who treated me like this?

Everything in me said NO. I really wanted to take that ring and throw it at him, but I didn't.

Even though it hadn't gone as I planned, I still wanted to be his wife.

"Why would you think it would be funny to make me wait all day, thinking that you hadn't even picked up the ring?" I sat on the bed, tears streaming from my puffy red eyes.

But I agreed to marry him.

And so we got married and bought the house and started our own little family. I tried to be a good wife and to make my husband happy.

But when Lauren started having problems, he spent more and more time at work, always saying that he was working hard for our future. I knew it was just an escape, so he didn't have to deal with our situation.

I needed help. I had no family and only a few close friends. When my friends did visit, most of the time they were there I was trying to console Lauren. I would also cancel at the last minute when we organised a get-together if Lauren was upset, as I knew it would be a waste of everyone's time. It didn't take long before my friends found that they were always busy when I tried to organise something to catch up with them.

I tried really hard to get my husband to see that I needed his help, but I never had any success.

"What time are you coming home?" I'd ask.

"Just finishing this job that has to be out in the morning," he'd reply. "We'll have a beer and then I'll be home."

"I've had the worst day with Lauren," I'd tell him. "It's seven o'clock and you said you would try and come home early again. Why can't you ever do what you say?"

"I'm going to be at least another hour," he'd snap back. "You wasting my time and annoying me isn't going to get this job done any faster."

"Fine! Whatever!" And I'd slam the phone down.

Most of the time it would go like that, devolving into an argument with me not seeing his point of view and him not seeing mine.

I was going to be doing this on my own.

Before Lauren was a year old, he was offered a job in Melbourne. By this stage, we had seen the best specialists at the Royal Children's Hospital in Brisbane and they couldn't give us any answers. I was told that the best neurologists and other specialists were based at the Melbourne Children's Hospital, so we packed up and moved to chilly Geelong.

I really liked Melbourne and the area where we lived. But despite its beauty, I was living in my own hell. We started seeing the specialists and once again ended up doing test after test. They couldn't give us any more information than any other doctors we had seen.

Lauren seemed to be getting worse; she was having constant seizures, screaming, and not sleeping. I felt so alone, and the only support I had was from a disability support group for young kids. Lauren had her first birthday there, and as I blew out the candles on her cake, I couldn't believe I had survived a year.

It had been the hardest year of my life.

My home had become a prison I couldn't escape. My loneliness was overcoming me and I longed for someone to hold me and tell me that I would get through it. There was an empty void in my heart that craved some kind of love. Just some appreciation of what I was going through. Some kind words of support. Any acknowledgment.

My husband was closed off to our world inside the walls of our home. When he was there, he was disconnected from us and uninterested in what was happening. He was just home to eat, sleep and spend time with Bec, if she was awake.

I decided to see a counsellor to help me. I needed someone to talk to, to try to work through everything I had in my head about my marriage, about having Lauren, and the continuing challenge she was and the guilt I felt about not being the mum I wanted to be for Bec.

After a few sessions, I finally made the decision to tell my husband that I was leaving him, even though I had made the decision some time earlier. It was a lot harder than I thought to actually have that conversation, but I knew I couldn't carry on in the lie.

I planned for someone to look after the girls. We went and got fish and chips and then sat in the car talking, which was something we really didn't do very much. It seemed like mid-conversation that I told him.

"I need to leave. To leave our marriage and go back to Mackay. You aren't supporting me and the girls."

"So just like that, you're going to walk away?" he responded. "I knew it was a bad idea for you to see a counsellor. How did they put this idea into your head?"

"This is what I want," I said, "not what someone is telling me to do."

"You've never talked about leaving before," he said, and I could see he was getting angry. "Then, all of a sudden, you go to see a counsellor to help with Lauren, and your solution is to leave your husband. How does that work, exactly?"

"I've been feeling this way for a long time. You can't seriously tell me that you're happy to be in this marriage." Somehow, I thought that he would be relieved that he would be rid of me and Lauren.

How could he seriously think that it was someone else's idea? We had been arguing constantly in what little bit of time we actually saw each other.

"Fine," he told me. "If this is what you want. You always get what you want anyway." He turned on the car as he spoke and angrily started to drive, turning sharply at every turn and speeding when he could. He was pissed.

We drove back to the girls without saying a thing, the tension in the car almost making it hard to breathe. The drive seemed to take twice as long as it should have, and I had so much going through my head.

Oh, wow, I did it.

I couldn't believe I've actually done it. I expected him to yell at me more.

I didn't want him to stay in the house, so I guess I was hoping he'd move out. And I wished we didn't have to wait a year to get a divorce.

And I really couldn't believe he thought someone else had told me to do this.

Once we were home and the carer had left, he seemed to take it a lot better than I thought he had and even talked about getting a divorce and moving out. The car drive had given him time to think about it, too.

"I need some time on my own," he said as he picked up the keys and headed out the door.

After I heard the car drive off, I was relieved. I had finally been able to build up the courage to be honest with my husband and tell him how I really felt. And that was it – now I could move on and make a better future for my girls and myself. I didn't have to answer to anyone, or to fight with anyone.

But could I really do this on my own?

The whole thing actually seemed too easy. I hadn't thought he'd react like he did; I expected him to blow up and for us to have the fight of all fights. Ending this relationship with a hell of a bang.

Maybe he could see that we were better off apart and that this marriage wasn't working?

He didn't come home for over four hours, and I hoped that he was okay. Even though I didn't want to be with him, I didn't want him to get in an accident. When I heard his car drive in, I was both relieved and worried – I didn't know what was going to walk through the door.

"We need to talk," he insisted.

I quickly bathed the girls and put them into their pyjamas, imagining us doing this in a little house all on our own. As I tucked them into bed, I gave them the biggest hugs, knowing that this was the start of our new life together. I just had to get through this time, until he moved out.

We sat down at the kitchen table and he leant forward and held my hand.

What is going on?

A huge lump formed in my throat; I really couldn't believe that he'd just done that.

"I don't want a divorce," he said. I could see that he was getting emotional; it had been a long time since I had seen that side of him.

"I want you to be my wife," he told me. "I want us to work on this marriage. I know I haven't been the best husband, but whatever has happened, we can fix this."

Unfortunately, what I'd thought was going to be an easy transition was short lived. When he came back that night wanting to work on our marriage, I couldn't believe my ears. This was definitely not one of the outcomes that I had thought about.

"What do you mean?" I was so confused.

Where was this coming from?

"I think we should both do counselling and start fixing this. I'm not ready to walk away from our marriage."

I didn't know who the man was sitting there speaking to me was. I didn't recognise him at all.

Lauren started getting upset just then. I had never been so grateful to hear that noise, so I could take some time to digest what had just happened.

I knew in my heart that I was already separated, but I agreed to do counselling and try to make the marriage work.

The discussions we had over the next few months didn't make me change my mind about leaving; I knew it was the only choice for me.

I had tried to be honest and upfront in the past in order to end our marriage, but it hadn't worked. Months had passed since I first told my husband that I wanted to end our marriage, but I was no closer to getting the freedom that I wanted. I felt like I was trapped and I needed a way out. I couldn't keep living like this.

How was I going to get out of my marriage?

Nothing I am saying is getting through to him. I want out, now!

I started doing karate as an escape from my prison and to have some time to myself. When I joined, it was around the same time as a guy named Tom. We were both beginners and found it hard to keep up with the other fitter, more coordinated members. I found that I was really relaxed around Tom and he made the experience really enjoyable.

It was incredible to add fun back into my life. I didn't realise how much I had missed it. To laugh and interact with other adults.

I had put on weight so it felt good to exercise. I was a sweaty mess by the end of the class, actually we all were, but we sat around chatting for a short while before heading home. I was just extending my time away from home, but it felt good to talk and connect with other people.

Tom and I would quite often pair up in sparring, as we were at the same level. We got to know each other really well and it didn't take long before a friendship developed. He was the only friend I had. I told him about Lauren and my marriage problems and he would tell me about the problems he was having with his girlfriend.

We would sit in the car after karate and talk for ages. It felt so good having someone to listen to me without judgement. It seemed like forever since someone had actually listened to me. Just being on my own for a change: for the first time in a really long time, I put my needs ahead of everyone else's. Even if it was for a short amount of time.

When all my walls were closing in around me, when sitting in that car, I could be me. It was the only time that my husband would look after the girls so I could do something for myself. It was more than just meeting new people, building my confidence, and exercising.

I felt closer to Tom every moment we spent together, and I knew he felt the same. It was just an innocent touch and a bit of flirting. I couldn't believe that someone was interested in me. That someone would actually like me, just for me.

One night when we were in his car talking, we touched hands and then interlocked them together.

"I like you," I said.

"I like you too," he replied.

We leant in and kissed. I felt like I was a teenager again and had butterflies in my stomach.

I really liked having Tom in my life. Having someone on my side, to support me. But I should never have taken it to the next level. As much as I romanticised the affair, I knew it was the wrong thing to do.

My husband found out about the affair, through my family. That was when things got really messy, with everyone getting involved. Tom's girlfriend found out, too, and somehow she ended up talking to my husband. They continued to talk, so that they could stop any interaction between Tom and I. We still managed to meet up a couple of times, but he always felt guilty and told his girlfriend, who would then tell my husband.

I often got a slap on the wrist for being a naughty girl and not following the rules. I was disappointed that Tom, who I liked and had put my trust in, kept dobbing me in. I really wished I had done things differently, but I couldn't change the past.

Within a couple of weeks of my secret getting out, I packed up the girls and my belongings and moved back home. Sitting in the airport waiting to catch the plane with my girls, I was amazed that I had finally done it. I was finally leaving my husband and our marriage – and I was relieved. I could leave all of the turmoil behind me and make a whole new life. While I wasn't sure what the future might hold for us, I knew that I was making a huge step forward.

Because I didn't have much money, I lived in a little house next to my mum and dad on our family farm. I thought things would get better and I could move on with my life, with my girls. That was the plan, but unfortunately, things once again didn't quite go that way.

My husband decided that he would move up as well and, much to my disgust, moved in with my parents next door. When I made the decision to leave my husband and move back home, my family became very involved in my life. I had made some really bad decisions in my life leading up to that time and I knew I was trying to find my way.

My family decided that it would be a good idea to have a family meeting. Whenever we had a family get-together, we normally sat around the table, but this time we did our usual greeting and then proceeded down to the lounge room instead.

My dad does woodwork, so there is a lot of timber in my parents' house. He made the wooden kitchen table and the wooden dividers which separate the dining room from the sunken lounge. There is a large wooden display cabinet filled with ornaments, some of which my mum made at ceramics, and a huge number of crystal glasses. On each of the floral print, lounge chair arms are crocheted pieces. I couldn't remember if they were the ones that my Nana had made, as she loved to crochet.

The lounge room is roomy and there are windows all around, with a large window in the front which overlooks the front cane paddock through to the creek. It was always bright and airy in there. Above the windows are wooden panels, and along the top of the front window are photos of all of the grandkids. As I sat there, looking at the large prints of each of our wedding photos on the side wall, my stomach began to churn with anticipation of what was to come.

My mum leaned over and gripped her coffee mug as she said, "You need to find a way to save this marriage, because you can't possibly do this on your own, especially with Lauren the way she is."

I wasn't really surprised by what she said, but I knew this was not going to go my way.

I knew that they really did mean well and were genuinely concerned about me. Although I couldn't understand, when they knew everything that had happened between us, why they thought I should stay married.

"I know you have both made mistakes in the past," my dad added, "but you need to put that behind you and stay together."

Has everyone suddenly forgotten about everything I told them about, everything I've gone through over the past year?

"That's what I want to do," my husband said. "Even though it will be hard to move past what you did, we have to put the girls first. I don't want us to get a divorce."

What, all of a sudden he wants to put the girls first? He has never put the girls first.

I had been looking after the two girls on my own for most of their lives. I had proven to myself that I could be a single mum, even though I knew it would be difficult. In that room, I felt more and more alone. I wanted to scream at them:

I can do this, I have been doing this, I can't stay married and be with this man!

"What do you want me to do?" I asked instead. I knew it wouldn't matter what I said; nothing was going to change. "We've done the counselling."

The look that came from across the room from my family was not a pleasant one. They weren't happy with my response, and it was obvious that they didn't think I had tried, since I was the one who'd done the wrong thing and cheated on my husband.

"You both need to make an effort and build the trust between you again," my dad said, breaking the silence.

"I can do that," my husband replied.

"Can you do that, Melissa?" my mum asked.

"Yes," I responded. I looked at my sister, but she couldn't even look at me.

"You have to do this for those little girls," my mother said. "They need a mother and a father who are together. You've seen those kids who grew up in a broken home. You don't want to do that to your kids. Do you?" She wasn't really asking.

"No." I stared at the floor with my head down.

I just wanted someone to stand up for me, to have my back and support me, but it didn't happen.

I felt like a naughty five-year-old being scolded. I was in trouble for having an affair and embarrassing my family. My heart wanted me to stand up for myself, but I couldn't get the words out of my mouth. I just sat there, agreeing and nodding, knowing that there was no chance of reconciling.

I was done.

I couldn't be with this man, not when he was never there for me.

I had been to hell and it was a horrible place, but no one was there to help me.

My husband had vowed to love me in good times and bad, but he didn't. He wasn't anywhere to be seen.

Even though I had said that I would try to make this work again, there was no way I could keep doing it. I knew it would disappoint my family, but I had to do what was best for my girls and myself. I just did what I needed to do.

The next few months seemed to go by so slowly. I tried to stay in my own house and make it special for myself and the girls. Making gardens and planting vegetables. But there was a constant invasion with my husband coming in and we would always end up fighting. It was like a tug of war with Bec, as he never wanted to spend time with Lauren.

"Lauren is your daughter too!" I would yell at him.

"This isn't fair on her or Bec. When will you ever see what you are doing to them?"

He would constantly question where I was and who I had seen when I went to town, that was twenty minutes from my parent's farm. I felt like I was being watched and kept track of every minute of the day.

"Where have you been?" he asked. "It shouldn't have taken you this long to see Lauren's doctor. What else were you doing?"

"I got some groceries so the girls and I can eat," I said in my most sarcastic voice "You don't get to keep track of me. This is ridiculous."

You don't get to control me anymore.

I can do this on my own. I will do this on my own.

I couldn't keep living like that and decided that I had to get away from this situation and find my own place to live. It took a while to find somewhere that I could afford, as I was supporting myself and the girls, on my own.

It took me a while to get on my own two feet, but eventually I moved out, and I felt like it was the best decision for me and my girls. Lauren was one and Bec was three. We moved into town, into a small pink house, which was very fitting since it was a house of girls. We made our little house a home, and even though Lauren was still having seizures and wasn't sleeping, I felt as close to normal I was going to get for now. I was making friends and working again for the first time since being a mum.

I really enjoyed being on my own and didn't miss having a man in my life. I was free and easy and I didn't have to answer to anyone. I didn't have to ask for anyone's permission to do anything.

I did, however, miss having company, someone to talk to and be close to. It had been so long since I had had that in my life.

Even though I knew that I came with baggage, I had decided I was not going to let anyone in who didn't treat me like I deserved to be treated. To have my back no matter what and want to be with me, all of me, just as I am.

Did such a guy even exist?

Did I deserve to have that love?

Chapter 6

"Don't fall for me or I'll break your heart," I told the handsome man lying beside me.

"I'm just happy for us to have fun and spend time together."

It was a couple of years later, and I had gone out with some friends to celebrate one of their birthdays. Coming home, I was in a large taxi full of people going to the same side of town as me. I'd drunk a lot of alcohol before heading home and was happy to escape my life for a night. While in the taxi, I started talking to a guy sitting near me.

"What's your name?" he asked.

"Mel," I replied. "How about you?"

"Matt. How was your night out?"

"Great, celebrating a friend's birthday."

"You leave my friend alone!" interrupted a friend of mine, looking out for me.

"It's okay," I said, reassuring her that I was able to take care of myself.

"What do you do?" Matt asked.

"I am a mum firstly, and I also work at the hardware store." It didn't even occur to me to lie to him.

Matt didn't seem deterred, so I continued.

"Bec is almost five and Lauren is three. They are beautiful girls and being a mum is the best thing, but we have had our struggles. What do you do, Matt?"

"I'm a diesel fitter, so I basically fix mining machinery. This is my stop," he said as we pulled up outside his house – just around the corner from my house. I was a bit disappointed we couldn't talk longer, but he gave me his number as he got out of the taxi with his mates.

The next day, I messaged Matt and found out a bit more about him. I was worried about what he would think about me having two young girls, let alone one of them having a disability. When I told him in the taxi that I was a mum, I was quite drunk and I think he had a few drinks too. I wasn't looking for a life long partner, but it was still a concern. I had so much baggage from my past and I didn't know how this was going to affect my future.

I managed to find my courage and I asked him over for dinner the next night. Bec was sleeping over at a friend's house, so Lauren had to join us on our first date. This was going to test what type of person he was. He would either accept the challenge or run for the hills.

Matt was really lovely but unlike the type of guy I had dated in the past. Maybe that was a good thing. He didn't seem too fazed by the fact that Lauren was crashing our party.

Matt showed up at my house on his motorbike, which I thought was pretty hot. He was cute, which was great, as I couldn't really remember how he'd looked from the night before. I don't know if it was his aftershave or what, but he smelled divine and I was happy I'd asked him over.

I introduced him to Lauren, who got the biggest grin. Her face just lit up. He spoke to her like a normal three-year-old, which was something her dad and most other people didn't do. Lauren just kept looking at Matt, smiling like she was on a date with him; she was smitten, and I felt like I was the outsider on their date!

We had a really nice dinner together; I cooked chicken and noodles. I was on a tight budget, so it wasn't anything too exciting, but that didn't seem to worry Matt.

I put Lauren to bed and we chatted for ages. We were very attracted to each other – so Matt slept over. Lauren did her usual thing where she was up most of the night, but even that didn't bother Matt. I was in a good place in my life and I didn't want a relationship with anyone; I was just happy having a friend with benefits.

Matt went away to a wedding, and then a couple of weeks later he had another one. I wasn't sure if he was just saying that to stay away, but we spent a lot of time talking on the phone and got to really know each other. I kept telling him not to fall for me or I would break his heart. It seemed crazy saying that, really, because I was the one with so many reasons for him not to fall for me. I had the baggage of two small girls and an ex-husband who made my life very difficult.

We spent a lot of time together, and it didn't take long for me to have to eat my words and say that it was okay to fall for me now, that I wouldn't break his heart. I had fallen for him.

Matt was an amazing dad to the girls, and they adored him. It wasn't a very easy job, though, with a lot of sleepless nights and an ex to deal with. I had wondered how long his patience would last. But I was so grateful that it did.

The most amazing thing about being with Matt was that I could just be myself. There weren't any games: just honesty. I never felt the need to even look at another man; my heart was so full of love for this one. Honesty and trust weren't something I ever had in my life before; I thought it was all too good to be true, but it wasn't. I never felt that I needed to change anything about him; I loved him just the way he was, and he felt the same about me. For the first time in my life, I didn't have to be or act like someone I wasn't, just to be accepted.

Matt was so supportive of me and the girls. When the house I was living in sold and we had to move, we spoke about moving in together. We hadn't been seeing each other for very long, but we were spending most nights together anyway, so we made the decision to move in together. Matt even looked after Lauren and Bec while I worked on the weekends.

He saw Lauren differently to anyone else, even me. He could see past her disability and see the incredible little human under all of that pain and suffering. Matt spoke to Lauren the same way he spoke to Bec, and that wasn't normal in my world. Most people spoke to Lauren like she couldn't understand or was a baby, but not Matt. I just admired him for his compassion.

We were really happy. I loved being with Matt; he lit up my world and made me look at it so differently. He had such a calming nature and was just chilled out so much of the time. It was just what I needed and such a change from what I was used to. He taught me to see Lauren differently, because I could only see the screaming and not sleeping and medication after medication.

We talked about her medication; by that stage, she was taking about six lots of medications, for epilepsy and reflux, and to combat all of the side effects that those medications had. This one couldn't be taken with that one, so we had them spread out over the day. Since she wouldn't just take them, I quite often had to hold her nose and blow on her face so that she would swallow it, all while screaming.

It seemed like a vicious cycle, and when they recommended adding another one to the mix, we said enough. I had always done everything that doctors had told me up until then. It seemed crazy that she was on so many medications. So we made the decision to slowly take her off some, to see how she would cope. It was a very scary thing to do, but something had to change, and we decided that it was worth a shot.

Lauren did have some seizures while off the medication and still had some reflux, so we kept her on some of her reflux medication. But, slowly, we started to see her personality appear. This cheeky little girl had been drugged up to her eyeballs and that her personality had been hidden from the world. I felt like the worst mum for having done that to her for so long, but I was grateful to Matt for changing my opinions and letting me see the amazing spirit that he had been able to see in Lauren from the start.

It took months before she was off most of her medications, and as scary as it was at the start, I was so glad that we made the decision to do it. Instead of Lauren's eyes being glassy and without expression, her eyes began to sparkle. She began to smile, which we hadn't seen her do very much in her life. Her smile just melted my heart and lit up all of the people around her. Lauren began to express being happy, and even though she still had times when she would scream, she would show that she was sad first.

This was the first time I had seen Lauren's personality, and I had so much guilt for not giving her this opportunity earlier. If I hadn't met Matt, I don't know if I would have ever had the strength to stop, or even the possibility of stopping, her medications. I was happy to follow what the doctors were telling me and keep doing what I thought was best for Lauren. Please don't get me wrong; I was grateful for the help from all of the medical staff we saw, and there was a lot, but I didn't for one second think there was another option. I was just a mum making it through minute to minute.

It was definitely not an easy road with Lauren, but we did our best and we grew closer as a family. On New Year's Eve, Matt and I got the chance to go away for a few days, and while enjoying the sunset on Hamilton Island, Matt pulled out a ring.

"Will you marry me?"

"Of course I will!" I didn't need to think about it.

There was no doubt in my head or my heart that I wanted to spend the rest of my life with this amazing man. I was so happy to be engaged and make our little family whole. I hadn't thought I would have the opportunity to fall in love like I had. Matt wasn't a very romantic man, but he loved me unconditionally and I loved him the same way. I didn't need flowers and romantic gestures to know that he loved me. He would tell me every time he left or on the phone before he hung up. I don't know how I got so lucky, but I was grateful to be in love and about to marry my forever husband.

We got married in a ceremony on the beach; the girls were the flower girls. It was a beautiful day filled with so much love. Even though it was a small wedding, we were surrounded by our closest friends and family, and everyone supported us. Lauren had been awake for most of the night before the wedding, as we stayed in a motel, but that didn't change my day. It was just magical.

Bec even gave a little speech at the wedding to Matt, which was beautiful. It definitely brought a tear to my eye and to the eyes of most others that were there, knowing that she had a dad who would love and support her no matter what.

Now that Lauren was off her medication and living in a house filled with so much love, she began to improve on every level. It was amazing to see how much difference it made when the world around her was positive: her health improved and she began developing her skills. It wasn't an overnight transformation; she had to work on improving every day.

Lauren was ready to go off into the big wide world without me by her side and start school.

Will they be able to care for Lauren like I do?

What will they do if she has a seizure?

How can they give her what she needed with so many kids in a class?

It was a scary time for me, and even though we had meetings and plans in place, I was worried about the level of care that Lauren would receive while at school.

Chapter 7

"Look at my girl go, walking across the room in her walker," I said, praising one of the best teachers there ever was. "I can't believe you got her to do this," I continued. "You're amazing! Thank you for encouraging Lauren and pushing her to do her best."

Lauren had an awesome start to her school life; actually, just before she began school, she went to a program that started her off on the right foot. In those early years of Lauren in school, we were extremely fortunate to have an absolutely amazing teacher. She was in charge of the class with all the kids in wheelchairs, as well as those with high needs, so she had her work cut out for her. She was supported by some fantastic teachers' aides, and together they created magic in that room.

Lauren did more in those years than she had ever done before. Her teacher knew how to motivate and get the absolute most out of her while also supporting her. Lauren would walk across the room, which was really large, in her walker, and be so proud of herself. The smile on her face showed how pleased she was with her efforts.

Unfortunately, the school got a new principal, and the whole school environment changed. Where before you would walk into the school and the kids and teachers would both be happy, now it had all changed. The new principal decided it was a better idea to put the high needs students in classes with kids their own age. So instead of having students with similar needs in a classroom where they did similar activities that were appropriate for them, they were put in classes with maybe ten other students at ten different ability levels.

Instead of doing activities where Lauren learned hand-eye coordination, she was doing maths sums, sitting in the back of the class bored out of her brain. Lauren can be a smart cookie, but for me, her learning 2 plus 3 shouldn't have been one of her top priorities; learning how to give herself a drink was more appropriate and, in my eyes, much more important. But what would I know? I'm just her mum.

I often wonder how different Lauren's life would be if, by some miracle, we'd had the teacher that helped Lauren achieve so much for a longer period of time. I know that we'd be in a completely different world. Instead of just being cared for, she would be inspired and encouraged to achieve more.

We were extremely lucky to have some great teachers over the course of Lauren's school life, and many of them are still friends. But they could only work within the education system, which put so many restrictions on their ability to teach Lauren the practical life skills that she lacked. It seemed to me the education system really lacked some common sense.

At the end of every semester, we would get Lauren's report card, and it would always make me so angry. Lauren had the lowest mark in every subject, but always had an A for attendance and a raving review of how wonderful she is in the comments section. I would even tell the teachers to not even waste time doing it; don't give it to her or to me.

It was ridiculous. Honestly, I knew Lauren wasn't going to get a B in science, because she couldn't write. She didn't even talk to tell you if she understood what you said. If she had to endure the classes, so be it, but seriously, don't fail her because they were comparing her to every other student in that class.

At least Lauren was enjoying the social side of school and had some beautiful friends. Her best friend was Emily, who was the same age as Lauren. They started the preschool programs at the same time and continued to go through school together. Emily was also in a wheelchair but could talk, so she had to do the talking for Lauren, too. She was such a beautiful girl, and Lauren loved being around her friend. When they sat together, Lauren would reach out and hold onto Em, even with her hand dribbly after having it in her mouth. Emily didn't seem to mind, and they had a great connection.

When Lauren was seven, Matt and I built our dream house near the beach, a house that we all loved. Lauren loved the beach, and we modified a little garden trolley so she could sit in it and be towed down to the beach. She would put her hand on the wheel so she could feel the tyre and sand. It was a sensory sensation for Lauren, and she would eat sand the whole time with the biggest smile on her sandy face.

The only downfall was that Matt was working at the mines and had to stay in the camp out there. I missed him not being home but soon adjusted to being on my own again as I had lived it before. Only this time, it was only half the time, and I always had him coming home to look forward to.

We discussed having a baby and growing our little family. Matt wasn't worried if he never had any kids of his own; he knew that I had had my tubes tied while having endometriosis surgery. Having a baby would not be an easy fix, and it was not going to happen naturally.

So we went along to see a gynaecologist, who thought we had a good chance of IVF working for us. We started the process of testing and monitoring, and when it came to the day of conception, we went to the day surgery rooms and had to decide how many embryos to use.

"I think we should do two," I said. After talking to other parents about it, I knew that quite often it took a few goes to work. I thought if we put two embryos in, it would double our chance of it working.

"Oh, I really think we need to start with one," Matt replied. "The doctor said we had a high chance of this working, so if both take, are you prepared to have twins?"

"Yes, but if we only do one and that one doesn't work then we have to come back and do all of this again," I pointed out. "If we do two, then we're doubling our chances." I really hadn't thought about having twins and how hard that would be; I just really wanted to increase our chances of it working.

"So if they both work, you know how hard it would be having two babies?" I could see Matt was trying to get me to see his point of view.

"Okay," I said, "so what if we do one this time, but if doesn't work we do two next time to increase our chances?" We had to make a decision and I thought Matt was right; it would be hard to have twin babies.

I religiously did all of my injections on time, even though it was hard in the beginning. I would get Matt to give it to me, but when he went to work I had to give it to myself. It wasn't as bad as I imagined it would be. Then it came to the day we had to do a pregnancy test. Matt was home, so I peed on the stick and sat there waiting for it to change.

I put all of my energy into that little pregnancy test and hoped for the result to be positive. I sat there with Matt, looking at the little stick and wondering what it would be.

Please be positive.

Please be positive.

Show me two lines.

I don't want to keep doing these injections.

It seemed to take so long for those three minutes to pass, but when they finally did, that second line never showed up.

My heart sank and my eyes filled with tears.

"Maybe we just need to wait a little bit longer," I said as tears started to fall down my cheeks.

I shouldn't have built my hopes up so much, but I really want to be pregnant.

Of course, I am being silly; most people have to do this heaps of times before it works.

"It's okay," Matt said, holding me. "We can try again. Don't worry; we'll go and get Freddy and Mary out of the freezer and do it again."

He always knew how to put a smile on my face.

"Yes, I know. I just really wanted it to work this time."

I wanted to retreat to what became my favourite place to cry. So I had a shower and bawled my eyes out. I was devastated. I really wanted to have a baby. I was still scared of having another baby with special needs; it was always in the back of my mind.

My need to share a baby with my wonderful husband was so important. Matt didn't realise what he was missing – having a little human that is a part of you. Watching them grow up and being there to see their milestones. I couldn't even describe to him how magical it is to have a love that is bigger than yourself, for this amazing little person who is so dependent on you for their every need.

Days passed and I still didn't have my period. I started to wonder if maybe there was a little chance that I was pregnant, but I kept telling myself that I shouldn't get my hopes up. I rang the gynaecologist and the receptionist suggested that we should do another pregnancy test, although it should have shown up in the first one if I was pregnant.

So down to the chemist I went to get the test and quickly took it home to do it. Matt was at work but was due to come home that night; I didn't want to say anything to get his hopes up again in case it was another negative test.

I sat there looking at the lines and waited, feeling a sense of deja vu.

And then, there in front of me, were two pink lines.

"I'M PREGNANT!" I shrieked, because I was home alone and so excited.

"Oh, my god, I'm pregnant."

I sat on the bed and reality hit me like a bolt of lightning. I had wanted this so badly, and now that it had happened, I was a little bit in shock. I had been so disappointed after the first test that I had resigned myself to going through another attempt to implant the embryos.

I was over-the-moon happy but absolutely terrified at the same time – happy to be having another baby but so scared that there would be something wrong with this baby, like Lauren.

How could I handle another special needs child?

Will I be able to go through all of that again?

It will be okay; this baby has Matt's genes. It will be fine.

I had learnt a lot with having Lauren, but I honestly didn't think that I could start over and do that again with another baby, on top of caring for Lauren and Bec.

When Matt got home from work I was so excited to tell him. Before I said anything, I showed him the test with the two pink lines.

"Congratulations!" I told him, almost jumping out of my skin. "You're going to be a dad!"

"What?" he said, a little confused. "But the test was negative."

"I know," I said, "but I still didn't get my period so I called the doctor and they said to do another test. So I did and this happened." I pushed the test at him again.

"Oh, wow," he said, "that's the best news I've heard all day. We're going to have a little baby."

"Yes, we are," I replied.

I loved being pregnant and feeling this little human growing inside me. My belly grew each week, getting so big it was about to burst. I loved it when the baby started to move and we could feel it kicking and squirming around.

It was always at the back of my mind that there might be something wrong with this baby. We decided not to have the prenatal screening that detected problems with the foetus. It wasn't that I was in denial about what might be, but I hadn't had that option with Lauren, and even if I had, I don't think I would have opted out of the pregnancy. For me, it was a blessing to have a child, and if I were to have another child with a disability, I would have to deal with that. There was no point putting myself or Matt through that worry if we didn't have to.

I did, however, express my concern about Lauren's birth to my doctor, and they took extra precautions when my baby was due to be born. Instead of giving birth naturally, they decided it was best to induce my labour so that I could be monitored the whole time. I also opted for an epidural. Since I had my other two labours without pain relief, I was going to be prepared and get the good drugs.

After almost having Rebecca on the side of the road while trying to get to the hospital, and all of the drama with Lauren's birth, the third time around I was determined to do things better. I wanted drugs and whatever else they could offer. I was not doing it again just with gas. I was a little surprised at just how easy it was with the epidural and delivery. With no complications and an easy birth, we welcomed our beautiful baby boy, Riley.

Everything went smoothly with Riley; it was a relief that he did most things by the book and never had any trouble with his development. I was always looking for signs of something not being right, but thankfully it never happened. It was so different having a boy. Wow, that kid did not stop; he went flat out all the time.

Lauren, who was now eight, was doing much better, and she seemed to love having a little brother. Bec, on the other hand, really didn't enjoy him being around at all; she had never had a sibling to argue with before, so she was making the most of it.

Once Riley started walking and talking, Lauren went quiet. After all those years of screaming and crying, she went silent. When she would laugh, it would melt my heart, and she would often laugh at the most inappropriate times, like when a baby would cry. Maybe she thought they had nothing to cry over compared to what she had gone through.

Lauren did speak for a very short time when she was about six years old and said "Mum, Mum, Mum" and "Bub, Bub, Bub" She only did that for about a month and never spoke again. I always thought there was enough noise in our house and maybe she felt she didn't need to add to it. Lauren had proved that she could speak, but I longed for the day that my girl would say, "Mum, I love you."

I always knew that Lauren loved me because of the way she looked and smiled at me. Her whole face lit up and it melted my heart everytime.

Just before Lauren became a teenager, she had to have surgery for her scoliosis, which was deteriorating quickly. We had known for a long time she would eventually have to have the surgery, as her muscles couldn't support her spine. When I asked what would happen if we didn't do the surgery, we were told that she would eventually be so bent over that it would begin to crush her organs. So, with no other options, we went ahead, and they organised to have the surgery at the Royal Children's Hospital in Brisbane.

The funny thing was that I had actually had the exact same operation when I was 16. I had scoliosis and surgery was the only option that my parents had, too. I wasn't in pain with my scoliosis, and after the surgery I recovered very quickly. I was worried for Lauren, though, because she would rarely let me know if she was in pain, and she had such a high tolerance for pain, but I didn't want her to suffer. I was so upset when they finally took her to theatre, but she left for surgery with a smile on her face.

Lauren had the surgery on Matt's birthday. He came with us to Brisbane for the surgery and would fly home not long after. I was trying to be brave for Lauren, to show her that I wasn't worried, but I was petrified. I kept telling myself that she would be fine and that really the worst case scenario was that they damage her spinal cord and she does not have movements of her legs. She was in a wheelchair anyway, so the potential reward outweighed the risk.

That day seemed so long, especially since she went into surgery early in the morning. They said it could take over five hours, and that they would call when she was done. I must have checked my phone every ten minutes at least. We went out for lunch not far from the hospital to celebrate Matt's birthday, but I couldn't wait to get back so I could be there when she came out.

When we arrived back at the hospital, we waited for ages, with every minute seeming to last so much longer. Five hours passed with no word. Six hours, and still nothing. Then it was seven and eight hours.

Something must have gone wrong.

It is taking so much longer than they told us it would.

What's happened?

"Do you think something has gone wrong?" I asked Matt.

"No," Matt said reassuringly. "She'll be fine. They would have called us if there was a problem."

Finally, they rang to say that she was in recovery and everything had gone well. What a relief. She was in the intensive care unit with so many monitors and tubes attached to her; it was frightening to see my little girl like that.

I stayed with Lauren in the hospital, while Matt went home to take care of Riley and Bec, who had been staying at Mum and Dad's. My bed for a fortnight was a recliner chair with a pillow and a blanket. Needless to say, I didn't get a lot of sleep, but it didn't matter. We were in a room with six other kids, all with different conditions and in hospital for different reasons.

The nurses, doctors, and physios were all so great. They had Lauren sitting up in her chair only the second day after getting to the ward. I was so worried about hurting her, but I think she was happy to get up and to have a change of position from lying in bed. The clown doctors came and visited regularly and Lauren loved them. We also had a visit from a dog that came to see all of the kids.

Lauren's pain was well managed and she seemed to be doing very well. There were a few days where she was obviously in a lot of pain and even cried. It was rare for Lauren to cry. In the past, she would scream when she was in pain, but she was rarely sad and rarely cried. Lauren only cried tears a few times in her life. The doctors thought it was something to do with her tear ducts, but with everything else going on, they never worried about it.

For the first time in a really long time, Lauren was lying in bed crying tears. It broke my heart to see her like that. We quickly got her some more pain relief medication, but I tried to just hug her lightly so I wouldn't hurt her more. I just wanted to make her all better and go home.

Finally, the day came that we could go home. The hospital booked our flights; we had our clearance letter from the doctors, our bags were packed, and Matt was ready to pick us up from the airport. The physios from the hospital went through the procedure with us of how to transfer Lauren into the plane seat. Even though I was nervous about having to move Lauren on my own from her wheelchair to the plane seat, I was happy to be going home. Finally being able to sleep in a bed was exciting.

When we arrived at the airport and checked in, they asked when Lauren had had the surgery. I told them it was 12 days ago and she said she had to check with her supervisor.

"Here is the clearance letter from the surgeon," I said, giving her the piece of paper that said there were no problems and that she didn't need to check because the doctor said it was fine. "The hospital actually booked the flights," I added, backing up my case.

"I still need to check," she said, smiling at me.

I stood there, trying not to look at the many people staring at me for holding up the line.

It didn't take long before she returned and handed my letter back to me.

"I am really sorry," she said, "but our policy is that you can only fly 14 days after her surgery, so I can't check you in for this flight."

It felt like someone had shot me in the heart, as I felt all of the blood rush from my head.

"No, that's not right," I said, keeping myself calm. "There must be some mistake. I have the letter from the doctor and the hospital booked the flights. I didn't escape from the hospital and book them myself."

"I am really sorry," she said, "but there is nothing I can do. You can't fly for two more days." She motioned for me to move on from her counter.

Tears started rolling down my face. "What am I supposed to do?" I cried. "I need to take my little girl home. We just checked out of the hospital."

Images of me trying to lift Lauren by myself in a hotel room for two days started running through my head. I wasn't supposed to lift her other than to get her into her plane seat to get us home.

"Is there someone I can talk to, a supervisor?" I asked. "Maybe they will understand." I was getting pissed off.

"I'm really sorry," she said. "Really I am, but we have policies and we need to stick to them. You could try another airline, maybe?" Again, she gestured for me to move out of line.

So I gathered up our bags, pushed Lauren out of the line, and moved to the side of the check-in area. I was devastated.

How could this have happened? I have to get home – but how am I going to get there? I can't go back to the hospital, but we can't stay in a motel, either; I know I'd hurt Lauren's back if I had to try to move her by myself. And how can we afford to buy two new plane tickets?

It was all just too much, and I fell in a heap on the floor in the middle of the Brisbane airport and cried and cried.

And then I remembered that Matt would be waiting for us. I needed to call him.

So I rang the one person I needed the most.

"They won't let us on the plane!" I wailed. I was a blubbering mess.

"What do you mean?" Matt asked. "They have to. You gave them the doctor's certificate?"

"Yes, but they won't let us get on the plane. What am I going to do?" I needed someone to come up with a solution.

"Ring the hospital," he told me. "I'm sure they will help. They booked it all."

"Okay, but we already checked out."

"Give them a call and let me know how you go."

I reluctantly hung up the phone, hoping that Matt would somehow save me from this nightmare.

I rang the hospital and the lovely nurse that I had said goodbye to only a short time before told me that in all the years that she had been there, she had never heard of that happening. She told me that people left the hospital all the time before the allocated days were up and had no issues flying. She said she was going to find out more and would ring me back but suggested that I try another airline as the check-in girl had suggested.

By this point, I was a bit of a spectacle at the airport. People were staring at us: my girl in a wheelchair and me a sobbing wreck on the floor beside her. Only a couple of people actually came up and asked if I was okay. I wasn't. I just wanted to take my girl home and sleep in my own bed.

I loaded up the suitcases again and, struggling to push Lauren's wheelchair and carry everything, we went to the other airline. I explained the situation, still with tears running down my cheeks, but unfortunately they didn't have any flights going home today. There was one last airline that I could try, so again I loaded up and headed to that counter.

Unfortunately, they had the same policy and wouldn't let us fly with them, either. I decided my only hope was to find someone who had a heart at the first airline, the one that we had our seats booked with. We made our way to the service desk this time, and I put all of my trust in someone seeing that we needed to be on that plane, which would soon be taking off.

"I am sorry," the agent said, in the nicest voice, "but I can't let you on the plane. I understand that this must be really hard for you, but my hands are tied."

I walked away again, and this time I knew I wasn't going home today. I couldn't control the crying: I was devastated and exhausted. The one person who knew how to hold me and make everything better was over 1000 km away, waiting at the airport for me to arrive.

I rang the hospital again, but the nurse hadn't had any luck trying to get us home, either. The travel office was closed because it was Sunday, and so we had to wait until the next day before anything else could be done.

"Hop in a taxi and come back to the hospital," the nurse told me. "We'll get this sorted for you, I promise."

So I did. I cried all the way back to the hospital and held Lauren's hand; I was sure she would be just as devastated to go back there. I rang Matt and told him what we were doing. He reassured me they would sort it out and we would be home soon. I really hoped so.

They gave Lauren her same bed back; everyone in the ward was surprised to see us but could tell that I was upset over the ordeal. The nurses gave us extra attention and everyone in the shared room chipped in for pizza for dinner.

The next day they finally sorted our flight for later that day and we made the trip back to the airport. I was worried about checking in and hoped with everything in me that this time we would get on the plane.

We made it on the plane at last and landed safely back in Mackay. I had never been so happy to see Matt and hug him.

Lauren recovered really well from her surgery and it didn't take long for her smile to come back. She continued to improve and having a rod in her back didn't slow her down.

When Riley was five, we decided to make the move to Moranbah, the mining town where Matt worked, so our little family would be together all the time. It was a great place to live and Riley thrived there, but there weren't the services to support Lauren. We spent a lot of time driving the two and a half hours to Mackay to see her specialists and then back home again.

Matt would also come into Mackay a lot to go fishing, which he loved to do. We decided that when Lauren was in her final year at school we would move back to Mackay, as otherwise she wouldn't be supported with what she needed when she finished school.

We then got news that there was going to be a new government scheme rolled out soon to help people with disabilities. While it was exciting, I was also worried about what it would mean for Lauren.

What support would be available for her?

Would she still be able to go to respite while we are in Mackay?

How would this support her needs?

I had so many questions with no answers.

Chapter 8

"This will change her life," I told the planner. "Oh, my god! You have no idea how much this means to us." Tears rolled down my face. "Thank you. Thank you so much."

"Just doing my job," the NDIS representative replied, "but I am so glad we get to help you."

I was overwhelmed and grateful we had the opportunity to give Lauren the life she deserved. To be supported in living a life like everyone else without having to worry about how we were going to fund it.

When the NDIS rolled into our area, I was so excited. I had done a lot of research and gone to every information thing available so I could learn about it. Sometimes I would be the only one there, which was fine by me as long as I got all of the information on things relating to Lauren. I put so much effort into planning for it and so much energy into what this could mean for Lauren.

I wasn't sure what it would mean, exactly, but I knew that if we got enough funding, it would change her life. When we finally did the interview with her planner over the phone and he told me how much we should get in Lauren's plan, I started to cry. I must have thanked him a hundred times; I was so grateful, and it felt like all of my Christmases had come at once.

I knew that if I self-managed Lauren's plan it would give Lauren more options but also create more work for me, which I was very prepared to do. It would give her the best year of her life, growing and developing her skills like never before. The planner in the meeting must have asked me 20 times if I was sure that I wanted to self-manage the plan, as it involved budgeting, planning and loads of paperwork. "Yes," I kept saying.' I had researched what was involved, and as I was responsible for all of the bookkeeping for my employer, I knew what had to be done.

Previously, the only support we had, had been some overnight stays at a respite house when we went to Mackay. A few months before the NDIS rolled out, we were offered four hours per week of care. I was over the moon when they told me I could have four hours; that was so much time to spend with Bec and Riley or go for a walk or anything, really.

Lauren was 16 at the time and was still at school, so we decided to do two afternoons for two hours. It was all done through a local agent in Moranbah and it was great having the extra help.

When we got Laurens NDIS package, it was like we had won lotto, but with it came a lot of responsibility. I was going to use every single cent of this package to improve Lauren's life. In the beginning, I didn't spend a cent. Instead, I researched like a madwoman.

We had recently received an eye-gaze device through the old government system. This device is a computer with a device attached so that it picks up where Lauren's eyes are looking and when she looks at something for a while it selects that for her, like a mouse would when you press it. When used correctly it will give Lauren the ability to communicate and navigate through the pages to tell us her thoughts and feelings.

We really only knew the basics of how to use it, so my first priority was to find someone who could help us figure it out. But finding a speech therapist who knew anything about an eye-gaze device proved to be more difficult than I thought.

I knew we weren't going to find anyone in Moranbah, so I went to the closest towns, with no luck. I had seen that people were using therapists with Skype as a possible alternative to face-to-face visits. I finally found someone who had limited but at least some knowledge, so we tried that. It was okay: not great, but better than nothing.

Thanks to the NDIS, now we could choose the people that were around Lauren and have the equipment that she needed to live a full life. We now had a brighter future – for Lauren, of course, but also for me, as it would give me the chance to work and to spend time with Riley without having to worry about whether Lauren was being cared for. I then turned my attention to support workers and how we were going to make that work.

Eventually, through trial and error, we found our feet with the NDIS. I loved the way this was going to change Lauren's future. Yet when I would get together with other parents, they would whinge about how they hadn't got all of the money that they wanted and how terrible the NDIS was. Mind you, they were never at any information sessions; they were too busy to make time to attend.

"Why weren't we given the same funding as Mary, she has the same condition? Why does she get more? That's not fair for Amy." I would listen to the complaints.

"Because it is all individualised, each person is different. Isn't it a good thing to have a say in Amy's supports?" I would reply, trying to get them to see the positives.

They were the ones who claimed that everything was against them, complained that they were punished because the NDIS hadn't given them enough funding. They'd say that the planner was terrible and the NDIS would never be able to continue to run like this, that the government would run out of money and it would be canned in a year or two.

Going from having little support from either funded supports or non-funded supports like family, I was grateful for whatever package we got. But now that we had the funding to support Lauren, I knew that the support available to us in a remote town couldn't compare to what was back in Mackay. We thought it would be better for Lauren to be where she would get the best services and more options when she finished school.

When we decided to make the move back to Mackay, we started searching for a house. We knew that we wanted acreage not far from Mackay city. I found a few but kept overlooking one with an amazing view; in the end, even though the house was small, we decided to look anyway.

Wow, the view was amazing. It overlooked the ocean, and I was sold just standing on the deck overlooking the five acres.

"This is incredible! The photos don't do it justice. It feels like the ocean is so much closer than I thought," I said to the real estate agent. Matt gave me the look, saying "Don't get your hopes up yet, we haven't even looked inside."

"It doesn't matter what it looks like inside, we would live out here anyway," I replied smiling at him.

"Look," I said pointing to the garden, "There's a bird bath and they have bird seed in that dish on the rail to feed the birds. How nice is that?" Matt again gave me the look. I was getting too excited.

"Let's check out the rest of the house," I said in my calmest voice.

As we walked through the rest of the house, there were more things I loved. The polished timber floors that went all through the house were beautiful. There was a huge oven, similar to the one that we had in our previous home. It had access to the verandah from the main bedroom and one of the other rooms.

There were things that weren't suitable, like the main bathroom had the smallest shower. There were no cupboards in any of the bathrooms and the kids rooms, only a walk in wardrobe in our room and some shelves in the laundry. We would have to downsize all of our belongings, as there was no way all of our possessions were going to fit into this house.

The house was nice, but had only three bedrooms. Bec either had to move out or share a room with Lauren, which was not a great option. I felt such a connection to the place and I was in love. I think Matt was too; his inner farmer was at home. We purchased the property and moved in. I had never felt so truly happy living anywhere, and I loved turning into my driveway, knowing this was my home.

The house wasn't suitable for Lauren, but as with everything throughout her life, we made do. We made a temporary ramp; though we tried so many ways to fit her in the tiny shower, we ended up giving her a sponge bath in bed.

After moving back to Mackay in Lauren's final year in school, my next mission in life was to find suitable carers for Lauren. I needed to ensure that she would be looked after when she finished school, and so that I could continue working.

It took a bit to work out exactly what I was looking for, and eventually I decided that I would just hire our own carers rather than going through an organisation. It was the best decision I had ever made.

At each interview I would ask the same questions.

"Why do you want to be Lauren's carer?" I would ask.

Most would answer with something like, "I think that all special needs kids are beautiful and I have always wanted to work as a support worker. I want to help people to achieve a happy life."

What they said didn't matter to me as much as the way that they interacted with Lauren. If they spoke to me or her, and how Lauren reacted to them. When Lauren looked at them and smiled, I knew that I had to ask more questions.

"What do you like to do for fun?" I always wanted to know how they have fun and how Lauren could be incorporated into that. I want Lauren to have fun and enjoy her life, but I also want the carer to have fun and enjoy their time with her.

Lauren's first carer was beautiful and just hit it off with Lauren from the start. She would sing to Lauren, and as she wasn't much older, they would do things that were more appropriate for Lauren's age. It was really important to me that Lauren wasn't with people my age all the time. She needed to have people around her who shared similar interests, so she could join in activities that most people her age did.

We had a few carers who really weren't suited to Lauren's personality, and it took me a while to learn to trust my gut when it came to the people who would be looking after my daughter. As a mum, it is a difficult thing to let go of that control and have someone take over the role that you had been doing so well for her whole life.

I had to learn that no one would be able to do as good a job as I did, and that that was okay. It really didn't matter if they had another way of doing things, as long as Lauren was safe and cared for properly. Well, it was that way in the start, but as I got to grow Lauren's team of carers, I wanted more from them, then just looking after her. I knew if they had the heart and personality to make Lauren happy, then the day-to-day hoisting and feeding and everything else could be taught.

I found that when I taught one person really well, they could then teach others. We now have a team of five carers who I call Lauren's angels. They are the most amazing group of women and look after Lauren as if she is their own daughter or sister. I know that I can trust them with Lauren's life, I support every decision they make on Lauren's behalf. There have been times when they have had to make hard decisions, but they have always put Lauren's needs first and I can't ask for anything more than that. Now that she is surrounded by such positive and bright energy, she has improved so much.

The first of Lauren's beautiful angels entered our lives after she responded to an ad that I put on Facebook. She lived just down the road from us and mentioned in her application that she had experience in massage. Lauren loves a massage and she lit up when Kay first came to meet us; I knew we had to have her as a carer.

"Hi, I'm Kay," said this naturally beautiful woman walking towards me. "You must be Melissa."

She came over and shook my hand. "Yes" I replied, "Thanks so much for coming over on such short notice."

"Not a problem. And this must be the beautiful Lauren."

Lauren looked at Kay with a big smile, then reached out her hand to touch Kays. She had a sense of calm about her, very similar to Lauren's. It was like they connected on another level.

"Sorry I don't have much time to talk, but I'm looking for someone who can do a couple of days with Lauren. Basically she needs help with most things like feeding and drinking. She doesn't have any behaviour issues and is really happy most of the time." Like most days in my life I was rushing to get somewhere, I didn't have time to sit down and go through the whole process like I did with the other people I interviewed. Kay didn't seem to mind.

"Have you done anything like this before?" I asked.

"No I haven't." Kay responded, " I saw your ad and I have been looking for something new in my life. Since you lived not far from me, I thought I would respond to your ad and find out more about it. The hours work in really well with my other commitments"

Kay was older than the other carers, but I knew I needed a mix of ages and skills. Each one bringing something different into Lauren's life.

"Lauren does love a massage. Would you be able to come over and try out for a couple hours one afternoon next week? That way you can see if this is something that you would like to do?"

"That sounds great. How about Tuesday at 3?" Kay said.

"Perfect. We can have more of a chat then. Sorry this is a bit rushed."

Kay seemed very keen and she spoke to Lauren for a while before leaving. Lauren didn't want to let go of Kay's hand. That was a good sign and I knew that she liked Kay.

When Kay walked into our lives, I didn't realise how much of an influence she would have on not only Lauren, but also me. Kay not only had great skills in massage, but an amazing knowledge of the body and how it works. Lauren and Kay had a real connection and I wished there were more Kays in the world.

"Poor little girl" are the words that I really hate the most in all of the English language. When people come up to Lauren and give sympathy to her and say that she is poor, it makes me mad. She is not poor; she doesn't need sympathy. She is happy and healthy. I know a lot of people don't know how to talk to Lauren; most of the time, they act like she is a baby or doesn't understand. Even though she may not speak, Lauren definitely understands what people are saying to her.

I think since the NDIS has come in, there have been a lot more people with disabilities in the community, but I live for the day when a person in a wheelchair going through a shopping centre is normal and no one really notices. Disability has definitely come a long way since the time when anyone with a disability was kept away from society and institutionalised, but I think we still have a way to go before there is complete acceptance.

When kids see Lauren they will often ask their parents about her and point to her. The parent normally tells their child that it is rude to point but never explains to them about disability. I love when kids come up and ask why Lauren is in a wheelchair. They are curious and want to find out about the world around them. Depending on the age, I generally just tell them that her legs don't work like theirs do, so she needs the chair to be able to move around. They don't need to know everything, just enough to satisfy their curiosity –

that way, the next time they see a person in a wheelchair, they will probably know that their legs don't work and move on.

It would be an ideal world where people would just accept others for being different. There are a lot of disabilities which aren't noticeable when you look at a person. But if we just accept that they are still a person with a mind and a heart and not be so judgemental, that's when we can change people's lives. I am fortunate that I don't have a disability – and the majority of people in the world don't – but the number of people with disabilities is increasing.

Maybe it's the food we're putting into our bodies, maybe it's the technology we have around us every day, maybe it's because we are so stressed out just living every day? I don't know. The reality is that there are more people with disabilities, so why can't we as a society accept that there are going to be more people in wheelchairs, more people with mental health difficulties, and embrace the fact that these people are a part of our world?

There are many things which annoy me about taking Lauren out into society, including people parking in disabled parks because they are only going to be quick and people saying "I'm really sorry" to Lauren. But my biggest gripe is when men, usually around 50–60 years old, use the disabled toilets so they can do a poo in the privacy of their own room, instead of using a cubicle in the men's toilets. As soon as that door opens and they step out, I know exactly what they were doing, and it wasn't because they needed the handrail.

So I have to take my girl in there, and so often I have to change her on the toilet floor because sometimes there are simply no alternatives. That's bad enough on its own. But when someone does that and stinks the whole room out just for some privacy... Go home and do it, if that's what you want. Don't use the disabled toilets. You would be surprised how often this happens. I used to give people the glare of my devil face, even when they wouldn't look at me, but now I say something.

I want to grab people and shake them sometimes, yell at them that there is a reason for disabled parks, and disabled toilets – it's because people who are disabled need to use them. I'm not the type of person who has little printed cards and puts them on people's windscreens when they park in the disabled parks without the sticker. I just hope that they don't have to use those parks one day because they have

Melissa Gorrie

had an accident and are confined to a wheelchair. Sometimes I think that is the only way people will consider their actions.

Chapter 9

Sometimes you are so busy living day to day, that you forget to take time out to check on yourself. When I finally did stop and look inside me, I found that I really didn't know myself very well.

I had lost my identity along this incredibly hard journey and I wanted to find the real me.

I had become someone's mum and someone's wife, but lost me.

I had lost how to stand up for myself, instead trying to fit into everyone else's image of how I was supposed to act and feel. I wanted to jump out of their boxes and show my true self, whatever that was.

I wasn't sure if it was because I had spent so much of my life just doing what everyone expected me to do.

I did try going outside of this box that people had put me in, when I was 18. I had a boyfriend who was 27. He was also a singer and a DJ so he really didn't fit into the ideal son-in-law image that my parents had. I really get that since becoming a parent, but at the time I was in love and he would tell me how wonderful I was and how great our lives would be. Soon after moving in with him I realised that this wasn't the fairy tale story that I had been telling myself it was.

He was doing drugs and drinking heavily, and he often was away a lot with his work. Sometimes when he got drunk, he would get angry and blame me for his mood, even though I hadn't done anything.

Once, as I walked in the door after a long day at work, Tom grabbed my hand.

"I have a surprise for you," he said, "it's in the bedroom. Close your eyes." I closed my eyes as he led me to the bedroom and I heard him open the door.

"Okay, you can open your eyes now."

When I opened my eyes, there lying on the bed, were three beautiful dresses.

"Wow, did you buy these for me?" I asked. I was surprised that he had gone to the effort of going shopping for me. They were absolutely beautiful with floral prints and long flowing skirts. I hadn't bought myself any clothes for so long, it was a great surprise.

He must really love me.

"No one has ever done anything like this for me before. Thank you. I love you." I told him with the biggest smile on my face.

"You deserve it. I love you too. I will always take care of you. You never have to worry, I will always be here for you," he said pulling me into his arms and kissing me.

It felt so good to be in a relationship and to be loved. I felt so spoilt and happy, but this feeling never seemed to last long.

A few days after he surprised me with the dresses, driving home after doing a late shift at work, I was looking forward to a shower and going to bed. I arrived home at 10pm and I knew I had to get up early as I had to do a morning shift at seven. It had been a busy day and I was exhausted.

When I pulled up in the carpark at the end of our group of flats, I could hear the music. My heart sank and I knew what I would be walking into.

I should just go somewhere else and sleep.

Where? Where do you think you are going to go?

There is nowhere else to go.

Just go in there and go to bed.

He will understand. You have been at work all day and you have to work in the morning.

It will be fine.

As I walked through the door, I knew it wouldn't be fine. He was drunk. Mel! mates were there and they were drunk. Probably off their faces too, but I was too tired to care.

"Mel!" Tom yelled so I could hear him over the music. "Great, you're home! We need some more drinks and I have run out of smokes."

"I just got home and I have to work in the morning. Can you turn the music down?" I said, knowing full well that I may as well talk to the wall.

"Come on, Mel," his friend begged. "I need some rum! I'm desperate and I can't drive. Obviously!"

"I need to have a shower and then I will see. Okay?" I needed to get out of the room.

I quickly went to the bedroom in our small flat. The music was still blaring, and all I wanted was silence. I had a shower and dressed in my pyjamas. I jumped into bed and put a pillow over my head to try and drown out some of the loud noise.

"What are you doing?" Tom said stumbling through the bedroom door. "You need to go and get us more drinks."

"I can't. I'm too tired. I have to work in the morning. Can you please turn the music down?" I pleaded.

"Who do you think you are? You come home, don't even come and talk to us, and hide in here."

"I'm tired! I need to get some sleep," I replied knowing it really didn't matter what I said.

"Fine! You stay in here and get your precious sleep. But I'm not stopping partying with my mates."

"I know," I said under my breath. Tom left the room and slammed the door. Even though I didn't think it was possible, the music became louder.

There was a second bedroom at the back of our flat that was separate from the rest. I decided to retreat to there in the hope that it might be slightly quieter. I locked the door so that they wouldn't come in. I knew from previous experience that I wouldn't be left alone.

With all of the noise I still couldn't sleep. I tried putting all of the doona and pillows over my head and put corners of a t-shirt in my ears, but it didn't help. As the hours ticked on, I counted down the time until I had to get up and go to work. Every hour was an hour of sleep that I badly needed.

"What are you doing in there?" Tom yelled at me from the door trying to open it.

I layed there in silence hoping he would just go and leave me in peace.

"Don't make me break this door down!" he yelled.

I was scared of opening the door, as I didn't know what he would do.

I was scared of not opening the door; if he did break it down he would be angrier.

I heard him talking to one of his mates outside the door, but with the music so loud I couldn't hear what they were saying.

I layed there so scared with tears streaming down my face. It seemed like I was waiting for eternity to see what they would do. But nothing happened. They must have gone back inside. I was so relieved.

Finally at 3am the music stopped and I finally got to go to sleep. Even though it was only for three hours.

I knew I needed to get out of the situation but I didn't know how. Tom isolated me from my family and friends, constantly saying that I didn't need them because they didn't support our relationship and the love we had for each other. So I had no support and felt so alone. He would yell at me and throw things; once Tom actually threw a whole cupboard down some stairs, smashing it.

When growing up, I had always been told that you should never let a man hit you, that is domestic violence and no one deserves to be treated like that. In some strange way I knew that if he ever hit me I would leave, yet I continued to put up with the constant verbal abuse and extreme anger.

There were times when I couldn't see a way out of the situation I had put myself in. I thought that if this was all my life was going to be, then I wanted out. When I was home on my own I took a sharp knife out of the knife block and held it to my wrist.

How did I get here?

How did this girl who had so much life, end up in a relationship where I can't get out?

I have no one who even likes me.

No one will even care that I'm not here. No one will miss me. I have nothing to live for.

But what if?

That little bit of doubt was the one thing that saved me, thankfully.

I finally did get out of the situation I was in and in doing so decided that everyone was right; you should stay inside the box created for you by everyone around you, because if you don't, bad things happen. It took me a very long time to put a little toe outside of that box again, and it was only a short time before I jumped straight back in.

When I was a teenager, there was no social media. I didn't have a mobile phone until I was in my twenties, and then it was so big, about the size of a small shoebox – definitely not pocket-sized. I am so grateful I grew up with ignorance of the world around me. I only knew what my friends told me at school, and the only news I got was from the radio or the evening news. Honestly, I was probably quite naiive about what existed in the world outside my door.

My kids, however, are growing up in a world where they are continually bombarded with comments and criticism, especially Bec. She was bullied from an early age in primary school, and although we made many attempts to try to stop it from happening, we never really had much success. I really just tried to support her, to get her to believe in herself and not worry about what other people think.

I tried to protect Bec and so didn't buy her the cool magazines that all her friends were reading. I knew that those magazines were full of photo-shopped images of beautiful girls on diets and the exercises that you should be doing to get a flat stomach. I knew because I had read so many of them and compared myself to the girls in them. I wanted their hair, their skin, their bodies, and the amazing smile with beautiful white teeth. As much as I wanted to set a fantastic example for my girls, that was just how it was.

When Bec finally hit high school, we gave her a mobile phone. But the teasing became worse, and she found that she couldn't switch off from the negative comments. This honestly broke my heart, because, as a mum I want to protect my kids and give them the best life.

We made the decision to move her to a different high school, and things seemed to improve. Bec started to enjoy going to school and made new friends. There were still issues, but it seemed like we were over the worst of it. That was the case until we moved to Moranbah. It was a really hard decision to move Bec from a school she liked and friends to a whole new school where she didn't know anyone, but we felt it was the best move for our family.

We moved a couple of weeks before the school holidays so the kids would hopefully make friends before the Christmas break, which both Bec and Riley seemed to do. The boys were interested in Bec because she was the new girl at school, and she liked the extra attention she was getting. But it didn't take long before some of the girls at the high school started being nasty and teasing Bec.

Bec came charging through the front door and I could hear her crying.

"What's wrong?" I asked.

"Someone wrote on the toilet door 'Bec is a whore!'" she sobbed while I hugged her tightly.

"Did you tell the teacher? Do you know who did it?"

"Yes I told Mrs H. I think it was Jane. She kept laughing with her little gang everytime I walked past. Maree told me about the toilets, so most people probably saw it before it was removed."

I tried consoling Bec, just holding her. "I know they can be nasty but you are better than them. Just let the teachers handle it and I will talk to the principal if I need to."

"I'm not a whore!" Bec said snivelling. "I don't know why they are being so horrible."

"Teenage girls can be horrible, Bec. You just have to stay true to you and know that there must be a reason why they are being bullies. Don't lower yourself to their level. I know it is hard, but try not to let them get to you."

I was so glad when Bec finished high school, she found some real friends when she started work. I am really proud of the young woman that she's becoming and everything that she's working towards. She has a lot to offer the world – she just needs the confidence to do it.

I want to show my girls and my son that they can love themselves just as they are. But why, why do I feel as though I have to look a certain way to like myself? This is not how I want to be and I know in my head that I should love the body I have. But when I look at my stretch marks, I never think, *Wow, that's the amazing result of carrying three beautiful children,* Realistically, my body isn't going to just bounce back into perfect shape after stretching to cover the little human growing inside me. Instead, I would buy all of the lotions and potions that were supposed to make me beautiful.

I had struggled with my weight since I had kids. When I was pregnant, everyone would say that it was okay to eat whatever you were craving because the baby must need it, or that you could have that extra piece of cake because you were eating for two. I had tried so many diets; each worked for a little while but never lasted. I had never really looked at why I was eating the food I was putting into my body or what it was doing to my body.

We always had people over to enjoy nibbles, followed by a huge meal and, of course, some creamy dessert that I really couldn't fit in, but it looked too good to pass up. I'd have an alcoholic drink at night because it had been a long day, or because the kids were driving me nuts, or just because I could. I never really drank a lot; I couldn't handle the hangover the next day and knew when I was getting close to that feeling that I should stop.

Sometimes in life you just have to look at yourself in the mirror, really look at the person looking back at you. To be completely honest with yourself and take a moment to analyse who you are. When I did this I wasn't happy with the way I looked. I had put on a few kilos, I had rosacea, wrinkles, and grey roots in my hair. If I were to be honest, I wasn't disgusted with myself, I wasn't obese or ugly – but I wasn't happy in my own skin.

Why can't I just be skinny?

If I just suck this fat off my thighs I would look better?

As I held my skin back on my face I thought *I probably don't need that much of a facelift.*

Pouting out my lips *I don't want duck lips.*

There has to be a way to get rid of this facial hair that doesn't involve waxing.

How do those girls get great eyebrows? Maybe I shouldn't have waxed them so skinny for years.

It was time to change the way I thought of myself and how I treated my body. I only get one body and it was time I started looking after it. Now I wanted to nourish my body with good food and, in the process, become healthy and maybe lose a few kilos. I didn't want to get sick, I wanted to give my body the best chance of fighting off any illnesses or diseases that came my way.

There were so many diets, plans and offers out there, and I'd tried so many in the past that didn't work for me. How could I know what to believe?

The internet overwhelmed me with what was the right information. I put the idea in the back of my mind to get back to it one day. But I wouldn't have to wait long for the universe to answer my questions.

Chapter 10

A friend of mine, Michelle started posting inspirational quotes and positive things that were happening in her life. It instantly got my attention, as it was not what she was normally like. Not that she was negative, but she never really expressed herself like that before. Then she posted things about these amazing products she and her son, (who went to school with Lauren), were taking and the great results they were having. I hadn't seen her in a while so we met up for a coffee one day with another friend and I asked her about them. They turned out to be just a naturally sourced multivitamin. I was already taking a multitude of multivitamins and everything else that was supposed to help me be healthy but I felt just gave me yellow wee.

I noticed a real change in Michelle, she was happier and seemed more positive than I had ever seen her. Her life seemed better and I felt drawn to that.

I was always looking at natural things that could help Lauren, but if it helped me too, that was a bonus. Michelle said that she had so much more energy. I could certainly do with more energy. I was always tired. Maybe I was still trying to catch up on years of no sleep, but by the time 3.30 pm came around, I was ready for a nap, even if I hardly ever took one.

I ordered some straight away and I was so glad I did. I was able to get some for Riley too, which was awesome. Michelle was right; I did get more energy. Instead of hitting the snooze button too many times, I was awake before my alarm went off – and I was able to stay awake and spend time alone with my husband after the kids went to bed, instead of falling asleep exhausted.

"Wow, I can't believe you are still awake," Matt said.

" I know, me either. It is really nice spending the extra time with you while the kids are asleep. I really don't feel so tired. Before I couldn't keep my eyes open." I said, snuggling into this chest.

"You would be snoring almost as soon as your head hit the pillow," he said smiling at me.

"Now I have lots of energy to burn. Anyway I don't snore."

"I know a great way to burn off some of that energy," Matt said winking at me and rubbing his foot up my leg.

I'd known for a very long time that I should eat healthier, but I never really made an effort to make that happen. I also knew that the produce I bought at the supermarket didn't have the same flavour or value to me, compared to those we grew on our farm when I was growing up. Dad used to talk about the quality of the soil and things they did to improve it, so I had a basic knowledge of what was good and bad.

The thing I didn't realise until I started taking these is what a difference it makes to your body when you give it the nutrients it needs. My energy levels started to lift, I went from really wanting a nap every afternoon and struggling to stay awake when I was driving home from work, to getting up early, having my own little dance party, and having to make myself go to sleep at night.

Some things took longer to notice than others; for instance, my hair seemed to grow more quickly and felt so healthy, like in those shampoo commercials where they flick their hair around in the wind.

The best thing is that I know I'm making my body healthier and that it's working on healing itself. If someone around me is sick with a sore throat, coughing, and snotty nose, I know that I have a really good chance of fighting off their nasty bugs. Don't get me wrong, I still get a runny nose and a cough on the very odd occasion, maybe once or twice in the colder months, but I find that it goes much more quickly than ever before. If I feel like I have a sore throat in the morning, by the afternoon, when I am driving home, I notice it has gone.

I added another natural product as well. My knee pain which I got whenever I walked up our very steep driveway, began to ease and is now gone. When Lauren started getting older and putting on weight, I started having back pain, some from when I had surgery for scoliosis when I was 16 and some from lifting Lauren when I shouldn't.

I actually still lift Lauren when I should be using the hoist to do it, but my back pain is so much better. I eased my back pain for years by taking anti-inflammatories constantly; at least every couple of days, but most of the time a few times a day just to keep on top of the pain. I was also on muscle relaxants from the doctor so that I wouldn't have to take as many anti-inflammatories, but I've started reducing the dose of these as well.

They also helped me with my brain fog; I don't have to have lists everywhere to remind myself all the time. I almost had to have a list to remind me of which list I need to look at. Instead of walking into a room and wondering what I went in there for, I remember most things quickly. When the kids were young I blamed it on baby brain; then, as I was getting older and forgetting things, I said it must be old age starting early. Now I don't need an excuse – my brain is working as it should.

Most times that I went past a chemist I would restock on anti-inflammatories and diarrhea pills. Having the runs was a regular thing, and I would always be on the lookout for where the closest toilets were, especially if I was eating out. I knew that dairy was a trigger for this, but there were obviously many others, as quite often it didn't matter what I ate. Not long after I ate, my stomach would start to churn and unbelievable pain would start. That was when I would take the first diarrhea pill. Then I would literally have to run to the toilet.

"What are you going to order?" Matt asked me as we looked over the menu.

"I would really like garlic prawns, but that's too creamy. Maybe I should just have a steak, at least that should be okay."

Matt smiled at me "You know it doesn't really matter what you order it will just go straight through you anyway." He knew me so well and he was right, most things I ate when out to dinner, made my stomach upset.

It wasn't pleasant, and it was becoming a regular thing, happening more than a couple of times a week. I knew it was like an irritable bowel, but I didn't want to have all the tests done to see for sure. A few people in my family have the same issue too.

Now I rarely get diarrhea and it is such a huge relief. I can eat out and not have to run to the toilet, unless I order something very spicy. I can enjoy meals and know that I won't pay for it later with the pains in my belly. I was able to fix it with something so simple – I just wish I had found this easy solution sooner.

By far the greatest improvement has been with Lauren. Seeing the results of her progress has been much slower, but I can definitely see an improvement in the communication between her brain and her muscles. She is following instructions and making meaningful vocal noises like she is trying to talk. There is still a long way to go; I really think that Lauren's body has a lot of healing to do, but it is definitely a step in the right direction.

I want to give Lauren every opportunity to have an amazing life, and I feel that if I can help to keep her healthy and happy, then I am doing great. It is not just the wholefoods that have helped her but a combination of that and the other therapies that we do with Lauren. We recently added some brain gym work, and all of these things help her to improve and develop her skills.

In the past, I tried different alternative therapies with Lauren but never stuck to them long enough to see the results. Now I know that it takes time to heal, and I need to have more patience in getting the results that we want in Lauren.

I've also found recipes which contain a lot of wholefoods and are delicious to eat. I realised that if I didn't like the food, I wasn't going to stay on track to be a healthier me. Once I got the idea of what was good for my body and health, I started to make up my own creations – things that were simple to make, because I'm not a gourmet chef and I didn't have time to make up fancy meals. I just wanted real food that was quick and delicious.

I decided that I would no longer listen to my brain when it told me I needed chocolate or soft drinks. My brain was just telling me that I needed something to satisfy me – but it didn't need to be food. I would drink water, take a walk outside and get some sunshine or have something healthy to snack on if I still felt hungry. I needed to retrain the way I thought about food. I definitely didn't live on lettuce leaves and kale, although I do love a good salad; once my body started getting the nutrients it needed I started to enjoy more healthy food. There are times that I do have treats, but it is a lot less often than I used to, and I don't beat myself up for it.

Only a year ago I was addicted to Pepsi Max, I loved it and couldn't make it through the day without it. One a day was initially enough to satisfy my craving, but then I decided that if I had one with lunch, I would reward myself after a hard day at work with another in the afternoon. When that wasn't enough, I would have another one with dinner.

I would crave it and couldn't live without a few Pepsis in the fridge, ready to go. I knew that it had a lot of things that weren't good for me, but it tasted so good. I constantly justified drinking it to myself by arguing that because I didn't drink coffee, I had to have some trade off.

But I knew that I had to stop drinking it. Slowly I reduced to two cans a day, then one can, until it finally was gone for good. It didn't happen overnight but I was very proud when I finally gave it up, even though the headaches, during the process, were very painful.

Water is one thing I love. When anyone asks if I drink enough water I don't even have to think about it. I always take a water bottle with me wherever I go, and I must say, I'm a little bit fussy when it comes to my water. I know there's a difference. I really don't like tap water – I can taste all of the nasties the council puts into the water. When I was growing up, I was lucky we had rainwater to drink, and we have put a rainwater tank in at our house so we can enjoy the nice water.

On the days when life is extra busy and I can feel my head starting to hurt, if I look at my water bottle and it's still half full, I drink the rest in one go. I don't drink soft drinks or coffee but might have the occasional tea in winter. I really just drink water all day, everyday. I know that my body is made up of a lot of water so I am really just refuelling the tank and feeling better for it.

After having such great results from natural products, I then looked into the business. I wanted to share what has helped me with others. I was absolutely overwhelmed by the support the community had for each other. I had never seen that before. They actually encouraged each other and cheered others on in growing their business while working on their own. It wasn't a competition; it was a team.

I found it to be so different to anything I had been a part of before. Everyone made me feel welcome, and I knew I was in the right place. I felt a real sense of belonging. I had tried a network marketing business before, but the products were so expensive and I really didn't believe in what I was trying to get others interested in.

I jumped all in with the business. I wanted to be part of such a positive community, since I had been lacking one for so long. I was really pleased to be involved in such an amazing company; everyone I spoke to seemed genuinely happy because they were. In addition they were normal people, not hyped up, just genuine and happy to be themselves and to help others.

When I got to meet these beautiful people for the first time, it was like I had known them for years. Everyone was so lovely and it was great to connect and be around so much positive energy. I loved hearing everyone's stories about how they were all looking for something to fulfill them in some way and how this business had changed their lives.

"I was a single mum with two young kids," said this gorgeous woman on stage. "I was struggling financially. I was struggling emotionally and I couldn't see a way out of my situation. That was until I met my beautiful friend Mary. She listened to me and helped me. My whole life has changed."

It wasn't just listening to one person's story that made me realise I was in the right place, but everybody's stories. The women that I heard talking in the bathroom about how happy they were. The amazing people who were brave and stepped outside of their comfort zones to be on that stage. It didn't matter about their past it was their future and their goals that was driving them.

All of these amazing people had different reasons for why they wanted to be successful, like giving their family more holidays or paying off debt, but they all had a yearning to change the situation they were in and more importantly they all had a passion for helping other people.

Like me, they wanted more from life. More than getting up and going to work week after week, struggling to save money and spend time with their loved ones. Even though I wasn't looking for a business this came at the perfect time in my life.

I found there was quite a lot of information on personal development in the business. There was a genuine desire from the leaders to help everyone in the community be the best they can be. I had actually done a bit of this in the past, but I always went back to the same old recording running through my mind.

While working on myself I found that my confidence grew and I started believing in myself. It made me think about my book that I started writing 10 years ago. Back then it was a book filled with information about having a special needs child. It was very factual and nothing much about my story. I felt like it was time to revisit this, but I had to change it and share my journey if I was to help others. I found when I started writing that it was more difficult than I thought to put my heart into these words I was typing. I needed to keep growing if I was to share my soul with the world.

I started listening to recommended audiobooks and I really enjoyed hearing them. Living half an hour from town and working every day, I spent a lot of time driving. When I became a sales rep for the company I was working for, I spent even more time in the car. I used that time to listen to as many self-help books as I could. I couldn't even connect my phone to the car stereo, so I took a speaker and listened to them on that. One of the audiobooks actually suggested listening to books on your commute; what a fantastic idea.

"Wow, what have you been on Mel, you seem to be bouncing off the walls lately?" Kay asked me as I walked through the door.

"I am really just high on life. I have been listening to this audiobook on angels and it is so good, I can't wait to keep listening to it," I replied beaming my smile at her. I knew she would understand what I had been listening to.

"I thought it might have been the moon, but you seem happy all of the time," Kay smiled back.

"I am. Really happy."

When I began to read and listen to audio books, it was like I was a sponge. I couldn't get enough new information. I felt like I was learning so much and just thriving on new knowledge. Some weeks I listened to 15 hours of audiobooks. Since I was never really a reader, other than Fifty Shades of Grey (which my husband was very happy I read), I was grateful I got to enjoy books in a whole new way.

Then I started to think about what I wanted in my life, not what everyone else wanted for me. It turned out that I wanted different things than everyone else. I just needed the courage to bring down the barriers around me. I started by letting people into my life - taking a chance and just going with my gut feelings.

There was a desire in me to achieve more. I knew in my heart that I wanted a better life. I wanted to help people, especially people with disabilities and the loved ones who care for them. I wanted to be financially free so that we could take more holidays and I wanted to have my husband home every night. I really missed Matt when he went to work and loved every moment that he was home with us.

I always knew I wanted more out of life, that I was put on this earth for a greater purpose than the life I was living. I was learning what was possible if I actually believed in myself. I had been a happy person for a while and wasn't really looking for happiness -just that missing piece I needed to make me whole.

I lacked the confidence in myself to achieve my goals. In the past I hadn't really succeeded at anything. The only medal I ever got was for an 800m run, and that was only because the girl that beat me every year was sick that year, so I got to win.

I'd start something but never believed that I deserved to be successful, so I would find excuses for why it wouldn't work or listen to people tell me how it wouldn't work -and then I would quit.

This is something that I still struggle with, but I made the decision that I do deserve better and that I'm the one who has to do the hard work to achieve my goals. So I started working out what my main goals are.

To have a successful business and help as many people as possible to be healthy and enjoy life.

To write this book, and in doing so encourage people to change their lives and live their passion.

To change the world of disability to be more positive.

My goals weren't complicated but they were authentically me. It didn't take long to come up with them; I had wanted to accomplish these goals for a long time. While I really enjoyed my job, helping people with their cleaning products was not going to fulfil my life's purpose and give me that life I wanted.

I began with the dreams I had. Bec had given me Kikki K's dream life book and journal and it was a great way to really have a good look at what I wanted in my future.

When I was much younger, in high school, my dream was to live in a castle and have a male harem. I think I just wanted to be treated like a princess in my castle but the idea of having a lot of men around sounded pretty great when I was a teenager with hormones I wasn't sure what to do with.

My dreams are a little different today. I knew that I wanted to put more emphasis into these dreams and make them my goals to work on in the next year. I knew it was great to have dreams but that they would always be dreams if I didn't make them a priority.

So I did a new vision board (I had done a few in the past) set my intentions, started my affirmations and hoped that all would come to me. I did a bit of work – definitely not what I could have been doing, but I still thought it would be enough. And then months went by and nothing much changed. My bank account hadn't grown any; my business hadn't grown very much; and I procrastinated about my book.

Why hadn't my world changed? I was doing everything that I had listened to. I knew that I wasn't going to give up on the business; I loved being a part of such a positive and supportive community, and I could see the potential. I believed in the products because they had changed my health, and I really wanted to help people with theirs, but why was it not growing like other people in our team? What was I missing?

I was 11 months into having my business, and yes, I made some money, but I wasn't where I wanted to be. I could have blamed it on a lot of things – the person who introduced me to the business was no longer doing it, and her upline who then supported me and was doing a fantastic job stopped doing the business as well. Some people who I'd sold the products to weren't getting the great results that I had and so cancelled their orders.

If I were to be brutally honest with myself, it wasn't anyone else – it was myself. I had to take a hard look in the mirror and realise that I was looking at this all the wrong way. It wasn't up to my mentors to hold my hand and tell me what to do all the time; it was up to me to support myself and learn from the amazing community that was there. My mentors had been there to help and support me when I needed it, but I needed to do the work.

Not everyone will get the results that I did; everybody's body is distinct and will heal in their own way, at their own time. I was the one who hadn't supported my customers or given them the information they needed to believe in the products like I did.

I was the one who had put up every roadblock that I could, just so that I could fail and show everyone around me that the box they put me in was the right size. It was me – just me, my thoughts, my actions, my life. I knew something had to change and now was the time to do it.

Kay opened my eyes to a beautiful new world, that I didn't even know existed. She never forced her influence on me; in fact it was quite the opposite, and it took a long time before I even saw her spiritual side. I started asking questions about angels and meditation and loved the information I got. I had always believed in God and heaven but I wasn't someone that ever went to church; I just believed in my own way.

I started listening to audiobooks on angels and was so inspired by them that I started doing meditations. I really didn't know what I was doing and found that for me, guided meditations worked better. My life was always busy and I found it really hard to stop thinking or to let my thoughts go. I was busy doing check lists in my head. I finally worked out that if I just let myself go with it, I got so much more out of it.

After seeing a post on Facebook about a group that was starting for people who wanted to develop and explore their spiritual side, I asked Kay if she wanted to come with me. We started going and it was a group of beautiful people, everyone was at different levels of their spiritual journey. Some were beginners like me and some were healers and a mix of in between.

The first night we went, we walked up these windy stairs to a house. We took our shoes off at the door and went in. I could smell the oils from the diffuser in the corner of the room. There were flowing curtains in bright colours and chakra charts and other spiritual pictures on the walls. The lights were dim but bright enough to see as we walked into the open space that looked like it would have been a lounge room, next to the kitchen where food was spread out across a table.

"Welcome! How are you both? I'm Julie," this woman started walking towards us opening her arms for a hug.

"Hi I'm Mel and this is Kay," I said embracing this radiant woman. She had long grey hair and a red skirt that swayed when she walked. She was so beautiful and I could feel her energy when she came close to me. It was like the first time I met Kay, I felt peace and at ease and I felt like I just wanted to absorb all of that light that seemed to beam from her.

"I am so excited you're here. Please help yourself to water, we will have the food when we are finished if you can stay and mingle." She looked over my shoulder as more people came through the door, "Hi Mary." Julie looked back at me as she held my arm, "so glad you came," and she moved to greet the others.

We started the group by all standing in a circle with our hands next to the persons beside us but not actually touching. Then we closed our eyes and Julie asked us to feel the energy that circled around the group. At first I couldn't feel it but then all of a sudden I felt like a warmth coming through my left hand, through my body and as if I was passing it onto the next person.

Oh wow that is really cool. Can't wait to see what else we do.

I loved going to this group once a month. I learnt so much about what is possible, about chakras and energy and a whole new world that I was only just exploring.

After a few months of going to this group with Kay, I wanted to know more and to explore the possibilities. There was a video on the groups Facebook page about a movie called *Emotion* that I watched.

Wow, all these different people saying that there was so much more to life. It really resonated with me and everything I had been feeling. In the movie, one of the presenters was Dr Joe Dispenza and I really liked what he said. Not long after that, I saw something about the book that Dr Dispenza had written called *Breaking the Habit of Being Yourself,* so I downloaded it and started listening.

It was the longest audiobook I had ever listened to, almost 11 hours, and I think because the author is a doctor and myself not being very sciencey, I found some of the book really hard to follow. I am glad I continued it, though, because there was information in it I needed to hear. I then downloaded the mediation that Dr Dispenza talks about in the book but I couldn't get it to transfer to my phone.

In the meantime, I was working on my business, trying to find these missing pieces to allow it to grow. One of the most beautiful, heartfelt leaders offered a group of support for 90 days. I had seen this leader talk before at an event and knew that what she was offering was gold, so I joined the group. A few days and videos into the group she mentioned how one of the leaders was using the meditation I had been trying to use.

I finally got it to work, and I knew that if I was going to do this, I had to do it properly and commit. The mornings were the best time for me, so I could have an hour of peace; I set my alarm for 4.30 and got up as soon as it went off. I had done some meditations in the past and had wondered if I was doing it properly. I knew when I was doing this one that I was; I felt as though I was no longer in my body and could feel my head nod like I was asleep. In the book, it says that nodding is a good sign that you are doing it properly.

The meditation started with breathing deeply and then my whole body floating. I then focused on the things that were holding me back from living my best life.

I want to change.

I don't believe in myself.

I don't believe I deserve a better life.

I deserve more.

I felt tears running down my face as I let these feelings go.

I then visualised my future; I knew what I wanted my future to look like, but I could see it so clearly and I was so grateful to be there in that moment when the dream became reality. I could see me typing away on my laptop finishing my book and standing up in front of a room full of people launching it. As I finish my speech I start to thank everyone that helped me and with a lump in my throat, that I just can't swallow, the tears falling down my cheeks.

I am then standing on a huge stage with thousands of people watching me, this time they are crying. After that I am dancing on the stage with everyone in the audience dancing with me. It feels like my heart is about to burst out of my chest, I am so grateful to be in the moment.

Then I am sitting in my bedroom which is now a story higher than it is, overlooking my pool and fruit trees, writing my next book. Feeling excited to helping so many people with my business and changing the lives of so many beautiful people. Feeling so happy to be able to make a difference in the world.

In the next part of this incredible movie in my mind, I am hugging Lauren, as I do every morning and she says "I love you, Mum." I am frozen in the moment by what she just said but I hug her a little closer and say "I love you too, Laurie."

Then Lauren and I are sitting on the beach not far from the waters edge. As I turn to her I say "Are you ready to feel the sand between your toes?"

"Yes", Lauren says with a huge smile on her face. "Thank you, Mum. I couldn't have done this without you. Thank you for believing in me. I love you so much."

"I love you too. Ready, let's do this." I help Lauren stand and support her as she takes a step towards the water.

"It feels funny on my feet," she says as she walks along the water's edge. I can't help but feel so happy that she is finally able to walk, tears of joy streaming down my face and I don't even notice the other people watching us.

I didn't want the movie to end, but I came back into my body and opened my eyes. Doing this meditation made me excited for my future and all that it can be for me and my family. The more I did the meditation, the clearer these video clips became in my mind. I became so passionate and excited to have these dreams come true.

My belief in myself changed -I knew that I did deserve the life that I dreamed of, that it was possible and nothing would stand in my way in reaching them. This time I would not sit around wishing for my future to get better, I was going to change the way I thought, change the way I spoke, and do the work I needed to do.

I didn't realise that this would be such a difficult journey. I now knew what I wanted, I could see it, feel it, hear it – but there were still roadblocks that I hadn't even imagined.

Chapter 11

The world around me, which I couldn't change, was the one thing that I hadn't considered. I couldn't make the people around me see my dream life. I could tell them how amazing it would be and go into all of the details, but for them it was just a pipe dream.

"There goes Mel on another one of those 'journeys', chasing stars she'll never reach."

No one ever said that to me, and maybe it was just my imagination, but I felt like the people that I really wanted to support me didn't believe in me. They didn't believe that I had it in me to complete this expedition.

I knew that it was only because that was what I had done my whole life. I had proven to everyone that that was how I did things. I start things but never finish them. How were they to know that I had changed, that this time was different? I had said to them so many times that this time is different, that I knew I could do this, but I never once proved I was telling the truth.

Even though at the time I would believe what I was saying, I just didn't believe in me enough to keep going and would give up. This time, I had to prove it. I knew that this time, my actions would have to speak louder than my words if I was going to get their support.

With that realisation, I decided that every time that a negative comment was made, it would give me more power to move closer to my goals. Yes, there were times where it really hurt and upset me that the people I loved didn't support me, but this time it was not going to stop me. It was going to be the driving force, keeping me motivated to prove them wrong.

I knew that most things that I needed to do were outside of my comfort zone. While it felt safe and calm in there I had to take risks and chances and just follow my heart. So I did take a step outside of my comfort zone, actually it was more like a leap, when I made the decision to do a tandem skydive.

I have always been afraid of heights, but leading up to the jump I didn't feel scared but more excited. Matt and my friend Nicki did the same jump in Airlie Beach a few years earlier and I saw how much they loved it. So my friend Les and I decided that we would do it together, but we kept putting it off and I was nervous about doing it then.

Since I had been trying new things and trying to experience more of life, when Les called about doing it, I was all in.

"Absolutely," I said. "I think I might be scared sitting on the edge of the plane, but hell yes, let's do this."

"Great! I have booked mine, you just have to book yours and we are good to go. You will have to help me, I'm really scared," Les said and I could hear her nervousness in her voice.

"Don't worry lovely, I will push you out if I have to. It will be great," I said, reassuring her.

So we met at Airlie and waited around in our skydiving gear, ready for the jump. It was the perfect day for it; the sun was shining and it was cooler weather. Matt and Les's husband David were there to support us and cheer us on.

"Ready to rock this?" my jump buddy said.

"Absolutely!"

I was surprised at how I hadn't become nervous while waiting there watching other people go up in the plane and float back down to the ground. I felt a sense of calm like I had never felt before, like I was outside of my body watching the whole thing take place. Les was surprisingly calm as well and when we were in the plane, all crammed in like sardines, the excitement kicked in. That was until the small plane started to turn quickly and I felt a little air sick. Once we leveled out and I could see the horizon, I felt better.

It was such a clear day and I could see the beautiful blue water and the magical Whitsunday Islands . All of a sudden there was a rush of air as they opened the door to the place. I must say that at that moment I was glad that I wasn't the person sitting next to the door waiting for the right time to jump. I could feel my heart beat faster but I still felt calm and excited for what was about to happen.

One by one everyone started jumping out of the door. I saw Les move to the door and in a moment she was gone. It was my turn and I was the last passenger on the plane. My buddy and I moved next to the door and as my feet went outside of the plane, I held my head back as instructed and then we were gone.

I'm flying

I could feel the rush of the wind but it was so surreal that it didn't even matter. I thought the earth would be rushing towards me but it really wasn't like that at all, I felt like I was suspended in the air and all I could think was how beautiful the view was. I felt calm and at peace. Maybe it was because I was close to heaven, but it was a feeling like no other I had ever had.

With a quick jerk the parachute released and the noise became quiet. As I floated down I took in every second as if it were in slow motion. We started moving around in circles and I did feel a little nauseous from that, but once we started gliding again that settled, thankfully.

"Hold your legs up," my buddy told me.

So with all my might I held my legs out straight as we landed safely on the ground. He unclipped the harness that was holding us together and Les came over to hug me.

"I flew," I said in a very excited high pitch voice with my arms flapping. "We flew!"

"I know," she said. "Let's do it again!"

"Yes," I told her. "That was incredible. Wow! I can't believe we just did that."

After we took off all of the gear and thanked everyone there, we headed out for breakfast. I honestly couldn't shut up, I had so much adrenaline running through my veins. I'm sure Matt was sick of me explaining every second that happened but I was beyond excited. It did take a few hours to come down from my high and every time

I think about it I can't believe that I actually jumped out of a very good plane.

I found that the more things I did that once scared me, my fears seemed to subside and I embraced stepping outside of my comfort zone. While I learnt that my fears were no longer holding me back, I knew I had work to do, and I would have to learn more skills and keep educating myself if I was going to reach my goals. I spent less time procrastinating and more time doing the work to get the job done.

I had done this at every job I have ever had, given my employer so many hours a week where I put in my best effort to work on their dream. Why hadn't I done the same for my own business and my own goals? Why? Because I was scared! I was so scared that I would fail -or maybe, that I would succeed.

I knew that if I stuffed up really badly in my job, that I would probably be able to find another job. But when it was my business and everyone was watching me, just waiting for me to fail, it was a whole other world.

I always valued what other people thought of me; I just wanted to fit in and not stand out in the crowd. I wanted to please the people around me, but how could I do that and still achieve my goals?

Honestly, I didn't think I could. It was a very hard decision to make, but I wanted my goals more than I wanted to make everyone else around me happy. It was my time to shine, my time to make my dreams reality. The time was now, to get to work and make my future the best damn future it could possibly be.

I couldn't control what other people did or said, so I was not going to waste my time or energy arguing with someone to get them to see my point of view. Everyone is on their own path and I have never lived their life. I have never walked a day in their shoes. I didn't know what thoughts they had in their minds. The only thing I did know is what thoughts are in my head; I control how I react to the things around me. It is just my thoughts that are concerned about what other people are thinking about me.

Sometimes it's obvious by what they say or do, but we don't know the reasons behind those feelings. They might be putting me down because they're jealous of what I have; I really don't know and am only guessing. We have so many thoughts going through our head every day that I bet most of those thoughts are about you.

We all think everyone is thinking about us and judging us, but most of the time they are thinking about themselves and how other people are judging them. How I see the world and the people who enter my world has a running commentary in my head. When I meet someone for the first time, I normally make a judgement based on how they look before they even speak. By the time that person leaves my sight, I have pretty much summed up who they are and maybe what they are thinking about me.

I am the one who controls my thoughts; I can stop the running commentary. I can choose to greet each person who comes into my life with love and ask why they are crossing my path, and maybe they can teach me something. Every time a negative thought comes into my head now, I say "out."

I no longer want to be that person, the one who is filled with so many negative thoughts, that it becomes all I see. When I put that negativity out into the world, that is all I get back, but when I change that to be more positive and happy, that is what I get back.

Yes, there are still grumpy people that come into my world, but it's how I think about them that has changed. I no longer get my back up and come back at them with their same attitude; instead I wonder what terrible thing has happened to make them this way and wish them all the best for a better life. Of course, this is done in my head because telling someone in a bad mood that you wish them well, doesn't always end with them skipping off to a new and improved life. I can't control how that person acts or talks, but I can control how I react.

It took me a lot of practice to do this, because when you've done something a particular way your whole life, it's really difficult to change that habit. The best way I found to start doing this was when I was driving. In the past, I was someone who was always in a hurry, and driving in traffic was frustrating.

I would be driving through traffic saying to other drivers, "Where did you get your license?"

"No of course you don't have to indicate, I am now able to read minds and I know exactly where you are going, you idiot!"

"Seriously mate it says merge in turn for a reason. Learn the road rules."

One day Riley even asked me "Why do you get so cranky with other drivers?"

"Because they don't know the road rules, mate. It's frustrating," I replied.

I then decided that when I drove I wouldn't be that person that I had been in the past; I would consider others around me, no matter what they did. I couldn't control them, only me and my thoughts.

When someone cut me off, I would gesture to them that they could go in front. It didn't matter if the car beside me was going to get in front of me and get to the lights one second before me; arriving at my destination one second later didn't matter.

"Yes, mate, you can go in front. I'm not in a hurry."

If someone was waiting for a break in the traffic so they could merge in I would indicate for them to go in front of me. As they give me a wave I would say, "You're welcome, you probably would have been waiting there for ages."

My whole driving experience changed, and I now enjoy driving. I am no longer the angry driver who abuses everyone for not knowing the road rules; instead, I have my audiobooks playing or music on, and my mind is focused on how great my day will be. I know that the other drivers haven't suddenly learnt the road rules and how to do everything right on the road, but my mindset has changed in that situation to be more positive. I am grateful for the time I have driving.

Gratitude is something that I never really thought about for most of my life. I wasn't grateful for what I had and was happy for life to just continue from moment to moment without any thought.

I am now grateful for everything I have in my life. There is so much in my life to be grateful for, and even though it has taken me a long time to see, I think having Lauren makes me grateful for so much more. She makes me grateful that I can walk and feel the sand between my toes when I walk on the beach. That I can speak and communicate to the world how I feel and what I want, because she isn't able to do that, yet.

I am grateful for everything that has happened in my life because it has helped me to become the person I am today. I appreciate my amazing body, which keeps my blood circulating and my heart beating and allows me to be able to move and think, because not everyone has that wonderful gift.

Being grateful makes me appreciate what I have and reconnects me with what is greater than me. Before, when I thought I needed material things in my life, it felt like it was never enough. I always wanted the next thing. It was a vicious cycle, until I stopped and really thought about what I do have.

When I looked at what I have and am grateful for, it shifted how I see the world. I actually see more of the world; I notice the nature that is around me, see the children that smile at me when I walk past and smile back. It has brought more into my life that I am grateful for, like the beautiful people that I get to meet.

Seeing the blessings that are all around me that I took for granted for so long makes my heart sing. Each beautiful sunrise and each flower that blooms is a blessing that most people don't even notice, now that I do, I enjoy so much more of what life has to offer.

I spent so much of my life focusing on what I didn't have, but I know now that being grateful is so easy to do. It doesn't take much time and brings so much to my life that I can't imagine going through my day without appreciating it.

I have started sharing this with my family and at the dinner table we go around the table and say one thing that we are grateful for that day. It really helps everyone think about one thing that brought them joy during the day. It doesn't have to be big, but it is a great way to connect as a family. Instead of focusing on negative things that happen during the day, it helps us see that even though some days are tough, there are still things to be grateful for.

"I will go first," I said, "I am grateful that I got to drive up to Eungella and see some customers that are so lovely. How about you Riley, what are you grateful for today?"

Riley sat up in his chair, "I am grateful that I got to have tuckshop and I met a new kid in my class today."

Matt joined in, "That's great mate, what was his name?"

"Ben, he just moved her from Melbourne," Riley replied.

"I am grateful that I get to sleep in my bed tonight and get to have dinner with my family. It's much better than being at camp," Matt continued.

"We are grateful you are home too," I said, smiling at Matt.

I easily come up with three things every morning that I am grateful for. In the beginning, there were days that I struggled to come up with three because they had to be different. Having the same thing every day wasn't going to make me appreciate the things in my life. Once I started, I could see there were so many things to be grateful for, no matter how big or small.

One thing that I am truly blessed with is my amazing friends. I have a lot of friends, but three girlfriends in particular are my rock.

A few years after I moved in with Matt, Ann moved in next door with her husband and three kids. They were Irish and the funniest people I had ever met. We would quite often spend a Friday or Saturday night or both having a few drinks and singing karaoke on Sing Star. Ann's kids weren't much older than Bec and their youngest was the same age as Lauren.

Ann would look after Bec and Lauren while Matt and I went to salsa dance lessons so we could do it for our wedding dance. It was a great surprise on our wedding night and it would never have been possible without my friend's help.

Not long after our wedding Nicki moved in on the other side of us with her husband and two kids. Nicki's kids were only a few years older than Bec so all of the kids spent lots of time playing together. It didn't take long before most weekends we would all be at one of our houses having dinner and drinks. We had so much fun and really enjoyed each other's company.

That's also around the time I met Les, who I later went skydiving with. Matt and I had gone out to dinner with a rep Matt knew through work, and Les was his wife. We had a great night and during the evening Les told me about her autistic son who was just diagnosed. I could relate to what she was going through since I had experienced some similar things with Lauren. We became close friends and as it turned out, Les just lived about 500 metres from our house.

Our parties were becoming bigger, but it didn't matter. We had so many great night together and everyone enjoyed each other's company. Since none of us girls had really even been away on our own without our kids or husbands, we decided it was a good idea to have a girls weekend away.

Our first girls trip was to Melbourne. Les was afraid of flying but once we were all sitting on the plane, Ann, Nicki and I were seated together and Les was on her own across the aisle from us. She was complaining about being her own and being scared until a cute guy sat down beside her. We all then offered to swap seats with her, as it was only fair that she didn't have to be afraid away from her friends. Needless to say she did survive the flight with the support of her neighbouring passenger.

I decided to surprise my friends with a limo ride from the airport to the casino, where we were staying. Once we landed we collected our luggage and headed outside to where the girls thought we would get a taxi.

"We should just say that we are the people for the limo and take that to the casino," Ann joked.

"I don't think that will work, Ann" I said walking in the limos direction.

"We will be fine," Ann insisted "just act calm, ladies. Pretend like we do this all the time."

"So what are you going to do when the real people show up?" Nicki added.

"We will be long gone by then, and drank all of their champagne" Ann said laughing.

"Where do we go to get the taxi, Mel?" Les asked.

"Just up this way somewhere," I replied knowing very well where I was going.

I stopped at the back of the limo. "I think we will take this, Ann" I announced.

"I was only joking, Mel!" Ann said confused.

"No really this is our ride, our champagne," I told them.

"Oh no, you didn't?" Les said.

"Oh yes I did!"

We all piled into the limo and laughed all the way to the casino. It was the best start to what was to be a great weekend.

The next day we all decided to go shopping. Because I had lived near Melbourne before, I knew that the shopping was great and only brought with me a change of clothes, pyjamas and underwear. I did however leave with a full suitcase and lots of new clothes. Nicki and Les didn't enjoy shopping as much as Ann and I did, so it didn't take long before they headed off in front of us. They called us after an hour of shopping and told us they were done shopping and were going to do a river cruise instead and would get some nibbles and drinks for us to have later.

A few hours and many bargains later, Ann and I returned to the room to find Nicki and Les had eaten all the food that they bought for us to share, and drunk the bottles of wine. Needless to say they were very happy to see us. Nicki shared with us that her husband and her were separating, so we decided to all go out for dinner and hit the dance floor to cheer her up.

It was one of the best nights of my life. I had never laughed so much and had so much fun. Ann kept asking the DJ to play All the Single Ladies for Nicki, but they wouldn't play it. She even followed the poor guy into the toilets to harass him to play the song. Ann had a dance-off with a much younger guy on the dance floor. Since Ann was a bit older, I'm sure the guy thought he had it all over this old chick. However, after Ann started doing the worm the guy admitted defeat.

When we finally got to bed in the early hours of the morning, we were all so tired.

"Goodnight girls, love you," Les started.

"Goodnight, love yous," I added.

"Best night, thank you girls," Nick said, half asleep.

"That was so much fun. This was the best idea. That guy was a good dancer but he just couldn't keep up," Ann laughed.

"You are too good, Ann" Les said.

"Let's do this again tomorrow night. It is such a great place to stay. Great choice, Mel" Ann continued.

"Good night, Ann" I said trying to get Ann to stop talking and go to sleep.

"I can't believe we get to stay here at such a cheap price. We don't need to go anywhere. Everything we need is here." Ann kept talking, "We need to make sure we do this every year, girls."

Someone moaned and Nicki started snoring.

"Girls? Don't pretend you are asleep. Okay I will shut up and go to sleep. Goodnight. Love yous"

Finally all was quiet and we got to go to sleep, ready for another day of fun and laughter.

I love these girls so much and would do absolutely anything for them; I know that they always have my back. It is so important to me to surround myself with people who lift me up and love me just as I am. We try and do a girls trip once a year and I always have the most amazing time. We go away and aren't anyone's mum or wife- just four friends having a great time together, enjoying each other's company.

There is so much fun and laughter that my jaw hurts from laughing so much. We stay up dancing the night away like we're still teenagers.

Sometimes in the past when I was in a group of women, everyone complained about how bad their lives were, how the kids drove them nuts -and then it became a competition over who had the worst husband. I felt uncomfortable then, and now in this situation, I would just leave or tell the truth, that I have a husband that I love and kids I adore, and that I have changed my life so that I enjoy every day.

The people who are close to you make a huge impact on your life, whether they are there for good or bad. When I am among negative people, it brings me down to their level, but when I am around positive people, it changes the whole atmosphere and makes me want to be better. Now I always try to be that positive person in the room - I want to brighten the days of the other people around me. When I do come across negative people, I simply stay clear or treat them like I treat everyone else.

I recently saw a small documentary on how having positive energy around things change them and had plants growing in an environment in which they played music that was happy and upbeat against music that was loud and had negative lyrics. The plants in the happy place grew so much more than those in the negative environment.

Now, I know we aren't plants, but I also know that surrounding Lauren with positive energy has improved her health and developed her skills. The mind is an amazing tool; it absorbs so much of what is around us. For most of my life, I thought that everything around me controls what happens in my life. It never even occurred to me that I should try and change the environment around Lauren to make her disability improve.

No one ever said I should look at what she eats because that could help her, other than to get her bowels to work better. No one ever took into account the things that were happening around her. With all of the doctors that we have seen over the years, not one single doctor looked at Lauren as a whole.

The neurologist looked at her brain, the physio looked at her muscles, the gastrologist looked at her reflux, and the paediatrician looked at the different aspects of Lauren's health, but not as a whole. Why is it that no one says, "let's look at the whole picture"?

As a parent, I was absolutely winging it; probably like most parents, I didn't know what I didn't know. I didn't have the time or the energy to look any further than the day-to-day grind. Now that I know what I know, Lauren can improve if the people around her believe that she can -if we tell her constantly that she is amazing and can achieve anything, and encourage her to do better, to take one more step even though she is over it.

Doing this changes how she thinks and what she believes she can do. It gives her determination like I had never seen in her before. Having the people around her think positively about themselves and their lives rubs off on her. It is like any of us: when you spend a lot of your time around someone who puts you down and treats you poorly, you start to become that person. You begin to believe those lies, even though you might know that they aren't true.

When I was with my verbally abusive partner, I believed that I was worthless and that this was the best I was ever going to get, because that is what I was told. Even though in between the fighting and yelling he would tell me that I was beautiful and a good person, the negative was much stronger. It didn't take long before that was all I could hear in my head.

I'd tell myself I'd made my bed, now I had to lie in it - that you only get what you deserve. I am so grateful now that I did eventually listen to that little voice in my heart that said I could do better.

In a few of the places I have worked, I found that there was one person who could change the dynamic of the whole staff. They would constantly complain, and I would even go as far as saying that they would manipulate people to get what they wanted. They would be the one gossiping about everyone else and stabbing people in the back. You could just feel the tension when you stepped through the front door, especially if they were in a bad mood.

I went through a time where such a person bullied me, and I hated going to work because of it. I wished for the days that she was sick and not at work, because when she was away the whole energy of the place changed. Everyone was nicer to each other and actually helped each other out more than normal.

When she left the workplace, everything changed for me. I enjoyed going to work and felt that I could just be myself. I didn't have to worry that someone was looking over my shoulder all day, waiting for me to stuff up so they could put me down for it.

Distancing myself from negativity and surrounding myself with happy, positive people just makes me thrive as a person. When I started my business and found that everyone was like that, it was incredible, and I felt at home from the very start. I have made so many more friends. I feel like the more uplifting people I have in my life, the more I attract these kind of people. It is like they see the sparkle and they come and shine with me.

Chapter 12

Time is the one thing that no one can control and most people just want more of. You can't buy time; you can't replay your time; it just comes and goes. When you really think about time, all you have is the very moment you're living in. You can't change anything that has happened in the past. That time has already gone, and you have already lived it. You can't make the future happen now; you can plan for the future, for sure, but you are not in the future. It will always be ahead of you.

So right now is the only moment you have, and you can control what happens in this moment. I have put a lot of thought into this lately because I seem to keep bringing up feelings about things that have happened in my past, and using those feelings to stop moving forward and achieving what I want in my life. What if the past was left in the past, and I just planned for the future and lived in the now?

My life was getting so busy, but when I broke it down to each moment and just made each minute count, it didn't feel overwhelming. It was just literally putting one foot in front of the other and living each great moment, still knowing where I wanted to be with the goals that I had. It really made me stop and think about the time that I was wasting.

I used to play games on my phone; I think I may have even been a bit addicted to Candy Crush and that Smurfs game. I was always checking when my next life would come or when the crops were ready to be picked so I could get to the next level. When I look back,

I think I could have used that time so much better -playing with my kids, learning something, anything.

I now look at my son spending time on all these devices and wonder where this will ever end. We always make sure that he plays outside and does things with us rather than spend all day in front of a screen. I don't think taking technology away altogether is something that I should do for my son, though, as this is the world he's growing up in. He plays online with friends that don't live near us and he doesn't get to see.

For me, it is about balance, and while that can be difficult at times, it's important to make Riley aware that there is more to life than the devices on which he is playing. He needs to be able to interact and connect with people you meet rather than just being able to send a message, to actually be able to have a conversation and to possess social skills.

Time is so precious. Making time for the ones I love is important to me, although I often think it would be easier if there were two of me for everyone to share. Matt is always saying that he wants more time with me, Riley wants more time with me, and Bec is forever saying that I don't make time for her. Let alone Lauren, as I think I don't spend enough time one-on-one with her. So how do I make myself stretch to meet everyone's needs?

"When are we going to spend time together?" Bec would ask on the phone. "You said we would have mother daughter time, but you haven't done it."

"I know honey, I'm just really busy. I want to spend time with you, but I have so much going on right now. I'm sorry," I replied.

"Stop saying sorry, you keep saying this but it never happens. Why am I always the last priority?" I could hear her getting more annoyed at me.

"I am trying Bec, let's make a time now. How about next Friday you can come over and have dinner with us. Lauren and Riley will be here but we can still talk. Riley can play his xbox so we can have some time together when Lauren goes to bed."

"Yes I guess, but we need to do something together, just the two of us," Bec said.

"I know, ok I will try to organise something. I love you," I said feeling guilty that I couldn't give Bec the response she longed for.

"Love you, too. Bye."

I simply can't fill everyone's cup, at least not at the moment. Right now I'm working over 30 hours a week, working on my business, trying to find time for writing, managing Lauren's NDIS plan and I do really enjoy a bit of me time. I just do what I can, and even though I am not meeting all of the needs of my family, I do my best to spend time with them.

Riley and I do activities after school, like going for a walk at a park before coming home. I try to fit in a lunch date with Bec when I can, and I try to do date night with Matt once a month. Lauren just gets mum cuddles every morning and I love that time with her. Being a mum is a hard job; everyone wants a piece of me, which I think is great. Even though I might not be able to give them what they want all of the time, the fact that they want more is actually really nice. I would hate it if my family didn't want to spend time with me.

I will be excited when I can leave my day job, even though I do enjoy it, as it will give me more time during the day. But I am more excited about when Matt will be able to leave his work and to come home to spend every night with his family and snuggle me while I sleep. While right now it seems like I am very busy -and I am, because I'm working on my goals and actually making time to do what is important to me -I know that it is so worth every moment that I put into it.

I no longer sit in the lounge and watch TV; my time is precious and doing that doesn't get me to where I want to be. Sure, there are times where I will watch a movie with Matt and Riley because we are doing it together, but watching random things on TV is no longer a priority in my life.

I rarely watch the news. There are hardly ever any good news stories; it's all about how bad the world is. Now, I am not so naiive as to think that everything is unicorns and rainbows, but to be bombarded every day with so much negativity is something that I don't have to do. I'm sure that if there's something that I need to know, that there will be enough people talking about it for me to find out.

Something I do make time for is dancing. It is what I love to do and it makes me happy, even though I'm not that good at it. When I would go out with my girlfriends, we'd always find somewhere to go where we could get up on the dance floor and strut our moves; if there wasn't a dance floor, we'd make our own. We would quite often be the first ones up dancing because we didn't care what other people thought about us; we were having fun, and that was all that mattered. There were always strangers coming in and joining in our little dance circle because people wanted to join in the fun.

I now like to start my day with my own dance party. After I do my meditation, I go outside barefoot on the grass and dance like no one is watching. Well, no one is watching because none of the neighbours can see, but even if they could, it wouldn't stop me. It lifts my mood and makes me appreciate how beautiful each day is when the sun is coming up. I dance around the plants in my garden and feel so much joy.

With my headphones in my ears, I would look up my playlist and hit shuffle play on my dance party mix. If it was a song that I wasn't into then I would skip it to the next song. When the music hits my soul and I can feel my body moving I then walked down the steps to the dance floor.

There is an open space next to the shed in our backyard. Surrounding the area opposite the shed is a garden bed with tropical plants growing. There is a large frangipani tree with beautiful dark red flowers in the corner near the deck. Near that is a dragon fruit plant that has branches coming off it going in all different directions. I always think that the branches look like arms and it must be doing its own dance waving its arms around. Tall palm trees grow behind the garden bed and often have bees and birds in them. The dew on the grass make my feet wet and a little cooler.

I boogie around moving my feet to the music, wiggling my hips and looking at the amazing trees and sky above me. It feels so liberating to be able to be free, to feel the grass on my feet and jump around waving my hands in the air. Some people think that I'm crazy, but for me it's just about having fun and starting my day in a happy way.

I can get so caught up in life that I forget to have fun, and adding a little bit of fun to my day makes a world of difference to me. I think there are so many expectations about how when you grow up you have to stop having fun and be a serious grown up. Whoever made up this rule must have lived a very boring life. Life is about living and enjoying every moment and having fun.

When I was a kid, I loved playing games and having fun with my friends. Then, when I got older, I was taught that you have to grow up and act like an adult. It seemed to me that the only fun adults got to have was drinking and sitting around talking. There was no playing.

It's okay as an adult to do things that make you happy, and that includes playing. We recently set up a huge tree swing for Riley -a tyre hanging by a rope from a large branch.

"It is heaps of fun, Mum; are you going to have a go?" Riley asked me.

"I will let Dad go first. If he survives I will give it a go," I said gesturing for Matt that it was his turn.

"Okay, I will have a go," he said, grabbing the rope. Off he went and he seemed to swing out a long way.

Making it back to solid ground he handed me the rope. "Your turn."

"Alright then."

Riley stopped me and grabbed a crate that he was standing on to swing from.

"This will make it easier. Just stand on this and then jump up so you sit on the tyre. That will be better." Riley seemed excited that I was going to try it. I normally wouldn't even consider it, but since I was changing my mindset, I was giving it a go.

OK hold the rope, jump up, sit on the tyre, hang on. I got this.

And away I went. "Woohoo!" I yelled as a sat on the tyre and flew through the air.

Oh no how do I get off!

I jumped off and made it safely back onto the hill.

Matt and I both had a few goes and it was so much fun, though after a while I was getting a bit sea sick and had to stop. It was liberating to be able to do something that I had loved to do as a kid and still enjoy it as an adult.

It is hard not to think about how fragile life is. I used to take life for granted. There are people taking their last breath who would give absolutely anything to have one more moment with loved ones. We don't have an expiration date; all we know is that one day we all die. If you were given five years to live, would you live differently? What if you were told you only have one year to live, would you change how you do things, see things?

Why wait? Why not live everyday as if it's your last day on earth? I'm not saying this to be morbid; the fact is that at some point we will all die, and we don't know when that will be. Only once you've had your 100th birthday will you probably know that you're closer to that time than a child.

I spent so much of my life waiting. Waiting for the right time. Waiting for the right person to come into my life to make me complete. Waiting for the perfect job to fall into my lap. Waiting for spring because it's too cold to go out and exercise. Waiting for Monday to start that diet. So much of my life was wasted just simply waiting. Don't wait for the right time. Do it now. There will never be a perfect time.

When I was young I wanted time to go by quickly so I could grow up and be able to do everything the bigger kids were doing. Then, when I did grow up, I wanted time to slow down so I could fit everything into my busy day. How often do we say that we don't have time? I think it's just a matter of priorities. If something is important to me, I will always make time for it. For me, as I've grown up, my priorities have definitely changed. I would never have thought a year ago that I would wake up early to meditate and visualise my goals, but here I am doing exactly that because it is important to me.

I want to make every moment of my life count by doing the things that I enjoy. By telling the people that I love exactly how I feel every day. By smiling and talking to strangers. I want to influence people to be happier and enjoy their lives, too. I no longer want to waste my life in a job that I hate, in a relationship that isn't loving, or by being around people who are miserable. Life really is too short, and while I have my time here on earth, I plan on making the most of it. Live in the moment and be present.

We seem to have lost the ability to communicate with each other because we are so involved in technology. It makes such a difference to people if you actually look them in the eye and have a conversation without being distracted. My kids live in such a different world; they find it hard to make friends in real life because so much of their time is spent communicating through a device. Don't get me wrong; technology is amazing, and because I have an online business I do use it a lot -and I've been very guilty of scrolling aimlessly through Facebook when I should have been present for my family -but there has to be a healthy balance.

When I die and go to check out, I imagine there will be list there of everything that some higher power had planned for me, my purpose for being put on the earth. I want to get there and be so overwhelmed that I have achieved everything on this list and more.

I did what society told me to do and didn't really think about what I really wanted. I finished school, got the job, got married, bought the house, went into debt, had the babies. What if I had died then? My only achievement would be my beautiful babies. I would have missed out on this amazing life. What if I had kept living that life, never stepped outside of my comfort zone, and died at 80? I would have made it to the end and checked off my list, disappointed about the life I could have had -if only I had taken a chance and believed in myself.

I don't want to get to my death and see the life I could have had and missed out on because I was too lazy or unmotivated. To wonder what might have been if only I had taken a chance and stepped outside of my comfort zone, if only I had believed in myself enough to do the things that scared me. What will be on your page, and will you be disappointed if you get to the end of your life and you didn't tick off anything in that amazing life that was waiting for you?

Chapter 13

Lauren is now 19, and I can't imagine what my life would be like if she were 'normal.' What sport would she be good at? What clothes would she like to wear?

It doesn't matter, and I never really think about how things could be different.

Lauren is an amazing young woman with an incredible outlook on life. She never complains about anything. She would have so many reasons to be angry at the world – for not being able to walk or talk or make choices for herself – but she never is. Her energy is happy and she smiles most of the time. She is happy to be here and loves the world around her. Lauren has a cheeky side, which has come out more and more the older she becomes. She laughs at all of Matt's dad jokes and says some funny things on her eye-gaze; when her carer takes her running, for instance, she will say, "Slow down, turbo."

Lauren also has a very sassy side where her teenage attitude comes out. When you ask her to drink her water, even though I know she doesn't like it, she will suck it up through the straw and slowly let it run out the side of her mouth. She also gives a great Elvis lip or blows raspberries when she doesn't agree with something. She's great at expressing herself without language. Her facial expressions and attitudes tell us a lot about how she's feeling, and she communicates that very well.

Every morning when I walk into her room, Lauren has a huge smile on her face and when I come up to kiss her good morning, she wraps her arm around my neck and pulls me in closer. When our cheeks are squashed together and I start giving her heaps of kisses, she giggles in my ear. I love hearing that sound and it makes my heart swell.

Lauren is slowly improving. She can sit on her own for a minute or two before she falls over. When Lauren is lying down, she can roll, but she can't get up into a sitting position, and needs someone to do this for her. She has improved, feeding herself with finger food and using a feeder with a spoon attached. When Lauren has a drink, she still needs help with grasping the handles, and quite often tips it up so that the drink runs out of the straw.

She is unable to use her wheelchair, so always relies on someone to push her around – hopefully they are taking her in the right direction. She is improving with taking steps in her walker, but Lauren is a long way off walking across the room, like she was previously able to do. She still requires a lot of assistance with everyday life skills.

She has an electric bed with rails which run all along the side. This is because when we had rails that only went three-quarters of the length of the bed, Lauren managed to wiggle her way to the bottom and somehow fell out of bed.

Even when she is in pain, she still manages a smile. Her pain threshold is very high, so she has to be in a lot of pain for her to let people know. When Lauren fell out of bed she landed on the floor, and I assume on her face as her nose was very red, but she never made a noise. It wasn't until the next morning that I found her, freezing cold on the floor and smiling at me.

"What are you doing down there?" I asked. She just looked up at me and smiled. "You're crazy, Loz. It's much more comfortable in bed." I scooped her up into my arms and put her back into bed to assess the damage. Luckily, from what I could see she was okay, just with a sore nose and a few bruises which emerged a day later.

I am really blessed to have such a wonderful daughter in my world. She inspires me to be a better person and to see the world through different eyes.

When Lauren was a baby it was so hard, and I could only see what was right in front of me. She is so good now that it is hard to think back to that time; it seems like a lifetime ago. Every time I come home from work or haven't seen her for more than an hour, as soon as I walk through the door she smiles at me, and when I come over and give her a kiss hello, she gives me a huge cuddle.

It was only a few years ago that I had to physically put Lauren's arms around my neck for her to give me a hug. Her arms would just hang there while I hugged her. Now she reaches out for me whenever I am within reach. When she does give me a hug, it is filled with so much love; she holds on so tight and won't let go. I have to physically pull her away now, ironically.

She sometimes even gives me a little head scratch or a back rub. I can feel her curly black hair against my face and smell the sweet scent of her shampoo. Her skin is so soft, the same as when she was a baby. The magical sound of her giggle when I tell her I love her is so sweet.

When we are so locked together, it's like we are connected on so many levels. It's like time is standing still and everything that we both went through in those early years was worth it to be in this moment.

When Bec was growing up, it was challenging because she was a normal girl, with normal issues like bullying and tantrums and attitude. She would yell at me and write nasty notes saying what a terrible mum I was. She would slam doors and constantly say she couldn't wait to leave home. Lauren never did these things. She may have thought them, and when she shows her attitude, I have to love that spunk about her because it is her personality. I can just turn around when she rolls her eyes at me and say, "Don't give me that attitude, miss."

She never yells back, "What attitude? I don't have an attitude!"

Never, ever. There is a reason I don't have that on her eye-gaze, although there is enough other language that she could use if she wanted to. But she doesn't.

I love all of my kids, but through all of the challenges she faces everyday, Lauren is so happy. She has a million different reasons to be angry at the world, but instead she chooses to smile and enjoy life. She still has her off days, like anyone, but it isn't very often that she speaks nastily to anyone on her eye-gaze. If Lauren is cranky at one of her carers, she will just ignore them or tell them to leave, but then she will be nice to the person on the next shift. The next time that carer comes back to work, she is all smiley and loving again.

She is the biggest flirt. If there is a man in the room she will bat her eyelashes and smile at him, though unfortunately most men don't really even notice, Lauren will try and grab them as they walk past to get their attention. She will often say on her eye-gaze that one of her friends is her boyfriend and giggle about it. I have to remind myself that she is a young lady and still has a body full of hormones.

If I didn't have Lauren, I know I wouldn't be the person I am today, and I'm grateful to her for making me see how wonderful life can be when you look at things differently. Instead of just living everyday without any thought to my future, I now appreciate the fact that I can walk and talk. I can feel the sand between my toes at the beach and dance barefoot on the grass. Everything that Lauren can't do, I can. I can share my thoughts and make decisions.

Even though it took me a long time to look at Lauren differently, I wouldn't be where I am today if I hadn't. I no longer see people as they are. Everyone has a story and are on their own journey. If Lauren had been born the same as most other kids, with no issues, and I had three perfectly fine kids, my life would be completely different.

I would be doing the normal mum thing with school drop-offs and pick-ups and lunches; instead, I was doing doctors and specialists and medications. I still did that with Bec and Riley, but there was always the extra pressure of Lauren's condition: her equipment and the continuing work, planning and budgeting her NDIS plan.

Lauren doesn't see people as different to her and really just likes most people. She is a very good judge of character and responds to people based on the way that they treat her, not on the way they look or sound or move. This is so refreshing, and I love that she has shown me how to do that.

I want the world to know not how difficult it is to care for a child with a disability but, really, how different it is to care for a child with a disability.

There will always be bumps on the road on our way through life, and yes, sometimes it seems like there is no way through, but somehow we manage to make it.

It's funny how, when you're preparing to have a baby, you read all of the books that tell you everything you need to know. Then the baby arrives and doesn't do what all those genius people tell us. What next? You need a new book! That would be the simple solution. I have tried to find a book that has all of the answers, but have realised that it simply doesn't exist.

Kids are different in their own wonderful way. Having a child that is a long way from the norm is a great thing. Lauren is unique and special and definitely one of a kind – and I wouldn't have it any other way. I am truly blessed to have had this special, unique little angel pick me to be her mum.

Instead of focusing on all the negatives that come with having a special needs child, I try to stay focused on the positive and enjoy the great things that we have rather than what we don't have. It's easy to get bogged down in life, especially when times get difficult, but I just think about how hard other people are trying and realise how lucky I am.

I believe that every parent should sit in a waiting room at a children's hospital, even if just for a couple of hours. You soon get to see how blessed you truly are and how many different people are dealing with situations so much worse than your own.

I always tried to meet up with other parents of kids with disabilities because I found that they were the best way to find information on available support or equipment. There were often support groups; some of these were great, and I made lifelong friends with other parents going through similar situations as mine with Lauren.

On the other hand, I found that some of these parents were incredibly negative and just focused on how bad everything was with their children or the person they cared for. It was like a competition over who had the most seizures, who had the least sleep, who had the most time at the hospital.

When I first went to these groups or events, I thought that that was how it was in the disability world and joined in the competition, coming up with everything that was going wrong with Lauren. When she was a baby, that was really all I could see anyway, so it didn't even occur to me to think of Lauren differently than any other parent in the room thought of their loved ones.

"Hi, how are you?" I asked the woman sitting next to me.

"Tired," she replied, "my son isn't sleeping lately. How about you? Do you have a child with a disability?"

"I know the feeling. Yes my daughter is disabled. What condition does your son have?" I asked.

"He has cerebral palsy. I am over going back and forwards to the doctor. We are trying to get his medication right. We are onto our third doctor and they have absolutely no idea what they are doing." This stranger was becoming agitated and turned to the woman sitting on the other side of her as she was leaning in to join the conversation.

"I know what you mean," said the other woman. "I have almost been through every doctor and we have just spent a week in the hospital because my son had an infection. They never cater for parents in there."

I always thought that most people in the hospital were okay, but maybe these women are right. They really didn't cater for parents. They really could have done better.

When the conference was finished I moved over to another group of women to meet them.

"Oh I can't believe Tommy is changing schools again!" said one woman.

"I know," replied the woman standing next to her, "God for bid he should actually get the help that he needs. His last teacher was terrible"

"How about you, hun?" the first woman asked me, "Do you have a kid at school? How do you find it?"

"Yes" I said "she goes to the special school. We don't have any other options with schools. She has too many needs for mainstream school."

"Oh I hope you have more luck with that school than me," added one of the other women who were standing in the group."

"Actually I better get going. I have to grab a few groceries before I pick her up." I made a quick escape.

It was the norm, and everyone just fed off each other until this big ball of negativity took over the whole room. I was part of it: it wasn't until much later that I actually opened my eyes and saw how much this affected my situation at home and how it had crept into every part of my life. I couldn't see the good in anything. At the time I was struggling to make it through the day and it wasn't until Matt came into my life that this started to change.

When Matt changed the way I saw Lauren and I started to focus on her and not her disability it really changed how Lauren's disability affected her. I can't begin to tell you how amazing it feels to have the whole energy in our house change from absolute despair to one of hope. It was like having a really shitty day and one of your girlfriends drags you out for a night out: as you're having the best time, you forget about all the bad things that happened during the day. Only it wasn't just one night; it was the start of Lauren improving her whole future.

I honestly don't know if I ever would have made it to this place if Matt hadn't come into my world. Maybe it just would have taken me a lot longer to get there on my own. Lauren didn't just wake up the day after meeting Matt and have a miracle cure. It took time – a lot of time.

I know that changing the environment around Lauren was a huge influence on her improving. Adding that positive energy and focusing on what she could do rather than what she couldn't made her able to do more of what she could do.

Seeing the smile and determination on her face when she is trying to take steps in her walker and feed herself is the best feeling in the whole world. Not that long ago I never would have thought this possible. It never even occurred to me that we might try these things; my focus back then was just on stopping her screaming.

It was a wonderful feeling when she finally did stop screaming, but it absolutely makes my heart swell up when she gives herself a drink with a modified cup and takes steps. Now I know she can do anything and I will never put any restrictions on what Lauren can achieve. Her future is full of so much hope and her dreams are her own. I will be there cheering her on every step of the way.

We still don't have a diagnosis for Lauren's condition or any answers as to why she is the way she is. There have been a lot of theories - that it was from her birth or due to her genetics – but now it really doesn't matter. Lauren is Lauren, no matter what condition she has.

I really wanted a diagnosis so that I could fix Lauren, but the doctors tested her for everything that they could fix. Apparently Lauren's case still comes up in discussions at the children's hospital as medical treatments advance, but I no longer need a label for Lauren.

When I go to meetings, which these days are mostly NDIS information sessions. I still hear everyone comparing who has the worst child in the room and who has it the hardest.

"Who do you go through to get your carers? I can't seem to find anyone that is good," said one of the mums who I had seen regularly at the special school.

"I am still trying to find someone that can actually show up when I want them too," replied another parent.

"The last ones that came to look after Jamie spent the whole time on their phone and didn't get to do half of the stuff that I asked."

She turned to me, "Who do you use? Lauren is always out and about."

"I find our own carers as I was having the same problems. It is extra work and has taken a bit to find the right people, but it is all worth it. We are blessed to have such wonderful people around Lauren." I said knowing that I no longer needed to join in the negativity.

"I couldn't do that," said one woman.

"Me either," said another.

"That's okay," I replied, "it's not for everyone."

Now I can stand up and say how grateful I am that Lauren is who she is and is able to achieve so much now that she is supported by such beautiful, positive people.

I really want to take these parents and shake them, to say that there is a better way if you look at your situation through different eyes, but I am not that mean. I want people to see that there is a better way of caring for a loved one with a disability, no matter what age, no matter what disability.

Chapter 14

When you peel back the layers on your body, you find skin, muscles, and bones. If you look closer, there are cells; look a little closer again and you'll find, we're all made up of energy. I learnt this at school, but it was very hard to believe since I could feel that I was solid and so couldn't grasp the whole concept. Instead of being these solid human bodies, we are actually energy. We are all moving around this world and it's own magnetic field, vibrating on our own different levels.

In researching how this all works, I found that our bodies have their own magnetic fields. The trillions of cells in our bodies are powered by electrical energy, and because the earth has its own magnetic field, this field influences our bodies. The food that we put into our bodies, the air that we breathe, and our environment all affect this electrical charge.

I can feel this energy when I am near someone that I love; it makes me feel at ease and safe. When I am around someone who is in a bad place, I can feel the negative energy. It's almost like getting a chill up your spine, or knowing instinctively to stay away. Having a connection with someone is being attracted to their energy. Needless to say I am attracted to Matt's energy.

When we are vibrating at the right level, because we are eating healthy and looking at our environment, our cells are healthy and allow our bodies to heal. While reading and watching all of this research, I started thinking about Lauren. I always believed that once there was damage to the brain, it couldn't be changed. Research has now changed that theory: it is possible to heal every part of the body.

Now, I am not a scientist, but I could see the science: if we could fix the pathways between Lauren's brain and her body, then she might be able to talk and walk, which would open a whole new world for her. For the first time in her life, I could actually hope that one day we might be able to achieve these things. It was no longer a dream; there was science proving that it was a possibility.

It all starts with vibrating at the right level so Lauren's body can do its job to heal. Since her body has been working this way for 19 years, it is going to take a long time to heal. But even if it takes her years for her body to rewire how those messages work, it will be worth it. We have nothing to lose and everything to gain if this science actually works. I wanted to give it a shot and do what was needed to transform Lauren's life.

A couple of years ago we started using Quantum Reflex Integration laser therapy on Lauren. When we added this to her other therapies including hydrotherapy, we knew it would be a long process before we started seeing results. We haven't received any miracles, but we are seeing slow defining progress with Lauren, and her fine and gross motor skills are developing.

We recently bought a PEMF mat and some other equipment to help with this, and we haven't had any amazing results since using it. I know it will take time, but I will keep researching and learning as science keeps evolving, continuing to work on Lauren being able to achieve what I once thought was impossible.

Something else that I have learnt about energy is that we have seven energy centres inside us, known as chakras. Each one represents a different vibrational frequency and colour and associates with specific functions that help keep us well. These are from the base of your spine to the top of your head.

When these energies have blockages from an event or feeling, then there is usually discomfort or pain. I have done some work with my chakras in the monthly spiritual group that I attend, but I know I still have work to do. When my chakras are clear and my energy is high, I feel better and much happier in myself.

The biggest step to finding my own true happiness was to like and then love myself. As a woman, I felt a lot of pressure to fit the perfect image of what society expected me to be. To actually look in a mirror and really love the person looking back at me was a hard thing to do. I had to see not my flaws but rather the beauty that was looking back at me. It wasn't about being vain; it was about loving and accepting myself as I am.

I had to stop pretending to be something I wasn't and instead find the authentic me and embrace that. It was okay to be different, and actually so much better to not have to play a role that didn't align with who I was. Much of my life I didn't know who I was, so it became natural to just be the image that society impressed on me - and then feel disappointed every time I didn't meet that expectation.

I was different in a great way. I have so much to offer the world, and I know now that I can help people, even in just a small way. I embrace who I am and where I am at in my life and look forward to what the world has in mind for my future.

Even though it was easy to blame others in my past for what happened to me, I had to take responsibility for my life and everything that happened in it. Every decision I have made in my life was my decision. Everything that happened to me made me grow as a person, and it was my journey that brought me to this incredible life that I love.

I had to forgive those that hurt me in the past to be able to move forward. All that baggage became heavier and heavier as I carried it through my life. Letting it go made it easier to go towards the things that made me happy.

While I thought I had worked through some of these issues, all I was really doing was pushing it down so I didn't have to see it. When something in my life triggered that memory, it all came back. All of the emotion of the past came flooding back to the surface, until I pushed it down again to subside until next time.

Actually facing each situation and working through how it made me feel, working through the emotions, was the best way I found to heal these wounds. It did take time and work, but it was worth the effort to let go of the baggage I had been hauling around for so long.

The universe has a funny way of showing us what we need to know, when we need to know it. For over 40 years of being in this universe, I was never open to anything spiritual. I had never really been around anyone that was like that, and the people that were spiritual were hippies that dressed in tie dye and danced under the full moon. I wasn't ready to see this side of me before I started opening my eyes to this whole new world.

I started noticing coincidences that were happening more and more. I would think of people for no apparent reason, and soon they would contact me. I would be thinking of something and that same thing would be mentioned in a song on the radio. It seemed like the universe was opening up pages to my soul one at a time.

I started learning about angels and slowly opened up to the idea of this world, where true peace and happiness are. If I had come across Dr Joe Dispenza's knowledge on rewiring the brain two years ago, I know I would not have been open to the concept and would have dismissed it without another thought.

Now that I am open to the signs that the universe is trying to send, I see them more and am experiencing the coincidences that happen around me everyday. I completely believe the law of attraction that what you put out into the universe you get back. When I am in a bad mood and put that out into the world that is all I get back. It isn't until I stop myself and change the way I think that this changes.

Now that I am aware, I trust in the signs that are around me. Recently I had to find a new carer for Lauren and after advertising the role, I was overwhelmed with the amount of response I received. It took a long time to go through all of the resumes and check the interested applicants social media profiles. The other amazing Angels all helped by doing extra shifts and working longer than they normally did. While they were happy to spend more time with Lauren, it was putting pressure on them that I didn't want to create.

Two women stood out from the others, so I interviewed them both and found that they both had great attributes and would be fantastic in the role. When they were to come and spend the day with Lauren to try and work out who would be the best carer, they both ended up being sick. I knew that it was becoming more desperate to find someone to fill this role and start training as soon as possible.

I felt like I was missing something and that the universe was trying to tell me to keep looking.

"What am I missing?" I asked Kay.

"I don't know but I feel it too," she replied. "Let's get out your tarot cards, maybe the angels can help us with a solution."

"Great idea. We really need to find someone and soon."

So I took out my tarot cards and pulled out all of the resumes. Kay and I did this together to see if we could find our perfect person to fit into our team of angels. I read the first card.

"Embrace your inner child. New friends or rekindled relationships. Children or childhood. Okay, that's interesting, maybe I need to look at someone that we already know. Is there someone that I haven't thought about?"

We needed more information. Pulling the second card from the deck, it showed us that it could be something from the past.

"Oh, maybe it is something from the past, someone we already know," I told Kay.

"Maybe we are looking at this wrong, let me see these cards again," Kay said standing over the cards laid out on the table.

"Inner child, maybe that means it is someone young like Lauren?" I could see Kay trying to talk her way through what she was thinking. "It would be good to have another younger person."

"Yes it would, but finding someone that can handle the role is going to be hard. It is a big responsibility for someone young. Let's see who we have in this pile that is young, that might be suitable," I said flicking through the pile of resumes on the table.

"Where do you come from again?" I asked Kay.

"Inverell," Kay replied, "why?"

"Because maybe it is from your past, not Lauren's. This girl is young and from Inverell."

"Let me see, I might know her family," Kay said as I passed her the resume. As she read through it she said, "She sounds great. I think you should call her referees."

"Yes, I think I will. Lilly sounds like a lovely name too," I said. "Let's check her on Facebook first."

So I checked her Facebook and called her referees and asked them if they thought she was mature enough to handle working with a disabled person. They told me that she was very responsible and trustworthy and would definitely recommend Lilly for the role. That she would be fantastic and I wouldn't be disappointed. They only spoke highly of her and I knew that we had to meet this amazing young woman.

When Lilly came for the interview she was just beautiful and her energy matched her smile. She was nervous because she had never worked in a job like this before, but I could see past all of the nerves. She was a year younger than Lauren but she spoke to Lauren like she was just one of her friends. I asked her to come for a few hours one day so she could see if this was something that she really wanted to do. It was just as much as a trial for Lauren to see if Lilly liked the work, as it was for Lilly to be able to handle the role.

As it turned out one of the other girls that I interviewed was feeling better and could come and try out to, but we only had one day available. As much as I tried to seperate the two girls the only time they could do was at the same time. So they came and tried out together, both knowing why the other one was there. The first woman had a lot of experience and was quick to jump in and help the other carers, as she knew what to do.

While Lilly held back in the manual handling times when carers were hoisting Lauren, she still interacted with her. Lilly was able to stay for a while longer and was left on her own on the verandah with Lauren. She was talking to Lauren, asking her questions about her eyegaze and really engaging with her. Lauren kept reaching out to hold Lilly and I knew that they had a real connection. When I rang Lilly to tell her she had the job she was very surprised and thought that we would choose the other lady who had more experience.

It was definitely the right decision. She has been amazing and has been a great contribution to the angel team. We are very blessed to have all of the angels that surround Lauren; they all bring different qualities to her day. They make it easy for me to live my life and let go of some of the responsibility in caring for Lauren. I put my complete trust in them and I know that they always have Lauren's best interest at heart. I will always support them in every decision they make on Lauren's behalf. I am truly grateful that they are here protecting my own angel.

I am more open to the people that come into my world and am much more accepting of everyone. Instead of judging others,

I find it better if I approach people with an open heart. Accepting everyone for who they are, instead of trying to fit them into a box, is so refreshing.

My instinct is something that I have learnt to trust. The gut feeling of whether to do something or not is something that never came naturally to me. I was always indecisive when making a decision. Always second-guessing myself and my decisions. But now I know what my soul says, and I trust that decision.

I love my crystals and want to learn more about them. They each have their own vibration and help with different feelings. I always keep some in my pocket or on me and I have them throughout my house. I also wear crystal jewellery whenever I feel I need it. When it is the full moon, I collect up all my crystals and charge them in the moonlight.

I also use essential oils to help with healing naturally rather than reaching for medications and going to the doctor. Knowing that these products are from nature and safe to use is great, but they also work. Riley will come and ask for a particular oil when he needs it because he knows it helps him.

I know that some people think I am a little crazy for believing in all of this, but maybe we all need a little more crazy in our lives. To believe in something that is bigger than ourselves.

Chapter 15

I really wanted to write this book to share my story with everyone and to show you that I am not anyone special. I'm not a genius, and I don't have any qualifications to my name. I have not always been the best parent, and my kids will vouch for that; I have not always been the best wife, daughter, or auntie. But I had a fire in my heart to do and achieve more, no matter what it took. If you have that fire, or even just a little spark, then you too can change and have those breakthrough moments.

I try to do just one little thing everyday that makes me smile or, even better makes someone else smile, too, because then the world will be a better place. These are things that have helped me to live a happier, healthier and more wonderful life that I love. I would thoroughly recommend everything that I have tried and still do because I want to continue growing and learning. There is so much more that I want to find out, but I also don't want to get overwhelmed with too much. I always have to make time for my family and the things that are important to me.

You don't have to spend a lot of money to find out what inspires you. There are books in libraries everywhere that you can borrow; now you can even borrow audiobooks. YouTube and the internet are great ways to expand your mind. I don't even have to go anywhere, just take notice as I go through my day of the things I'm telling myself, remember that little voice inside my head is controlled by me. Taking moments out of my day to think and feel is a great place to start.

While my husband would like me to be Wonder Woman, I am not a superhero. I just have a passion for helping people and I want the best life I can possibly have. When I look back on my life -and writing this book has really put a magnifying glass on some of it -I don't regret anything. I wouldn't change a thing in my past, as everything I have been through has brought me to this very moment and has made me the person I am today.

There have been times in my life that I wanted to give up; when I couldn't see a better future; but there is a reason that I got through every single moment. The things that were the hardest to go through definitely made me stronger and have given me the ability to know that I can achieve amazing things in my life.

I don't hate the people in my past that hurt me. While it took a long time to let that go, I am actually thankful to them for giving me the lessons that I needed to get me to where I am. I may not have known it at the time, but now I can see that I had to go through the hard times to appreciate the great times. I had to grow as a person and learn the life lessons that I did on my journey to being here right now in this moment.

I know that I am a great mum and a great wife; there are still times when I question my parenting skills, but I am doing my absolute best. While others may look at me and think I have everything together, I still struggle to balance my life and give my family the best of me. I don't believe there is such a thing as being perfect.

I used to look with envy at other parents who always seemed so calm and together, but after speaking to them I realised that they too, were struggling. We don't have to be perfect for anyone. While it took me a while to realise, I think deep down we would all just like to be accepted and loved as we are. I no longer need to compare myself to others and can just accept that I am a long way from perfect. And that is okay.

My life has been an incredible journey, and I have grown so much. I have overcome more than I thought I would be able to handle and come out happier and more positive and than I could ever have thought possible. No matter what life gives you, learn and grow from it. Keep moving forward into the world that you want.

You have everything in you to achieve whatever you want to. You just have to decide what you truly want. That passion in your heart that doesn't go away because you're having a bad day, or even a bad year. Listen to what your heart is telling you and block out all of the negative talk inside your head trying to talk you out of it. If you have that burning desire inside of you like I did, let it out.

Believe in yourself and start imagining the future you have always dreamed of. You deserve it more than you realise. Yes, it is going to be hard, and yes, there will be times that you want to give up, but don't. The only thing that is going to stop you achieving what you want in life is you and giving up on your dreams. While it is really hard to do, block out all of the outside forces that are trying to bring you back to their level -be bigger than them. Be bigger than the thought in your head that tell you that you can't do it, that you aren't good enough. You are.

All of the labels that you, others and society have put on you, peel them off. They don't define who you are. Under all those words and feelings, is the real, authentic you. It can take a while to find, but the true you is there and always has been.

I believe in you, and I will be your cheer squad in the back of your head, pushing you to achieve more. Unfortunately, I won't be there to call when you want to give up; it will just be you. I won't be there to do the work for you that needs to be done; that is up to you. You can have the best life coaches in the world who lift you up every single day, but in the end it's up to you. You are the only one who can change your situation.

You are the only one who can rise above every terrible thing that has happened in your life and become a better person. Even if you are doing it to prove wrong all those people who didn't believe in you, let that drive you to a better life. Find the passion inside of you and turn that spark into a roaring fire. You deserve the best possible life you could ever imagine; actually, you probably deserve more. Stop sitting around waiting for someone to hand it to you on a platter, because that is not likely to happen. No one is coming to save you.

I look at my journey of how I went from the hardest time in my life to being ridiculously happy, of being a part of the greatest love story and finding my power. The past year has been an amazing year of learning and growing. Discovering my soul and the amazing potential of my mind. There were times it was really difficult to pull back the layers and see the rawness that was hiding, but I am so happy that I did.

My life has been an incredible journey, but I know this is just the start to stepping into my greatness. For Lauren to grow and develop into a wonderful woman with so many lessons to teach the world. I am excited for every day, and I can't wait to share this amazing experience with you.

Acknowledgements

I am so grateful to all of the people who touched my life. Those who came and went and those who chose to stay and share this incredible journey with me.

To Cathryn Mora, my book coach, thank you for guiding me in the process of writing this book. For helping me change it from a simple story to one that I am very proud to share with the world.

To Karina Low, you are an inspirational woman who showed me that it is possible to reach your goals if you don't ever give up.

To Les, Nicki and Ann, thank you my beautiful friends for always being there for me. For showing me what real friendship is and making me laugh so hard that I just can't stop.

To Kay, my lovely soul sister, thank you for appearing in my world and showing me that the world is bigger than what I can see and touch.

To Riley, you are an amazing young man and I am so proud to be your mum. Reach for the stars and follow your dreams.

To Bec, I am so proud of you and all that you have achieved. You will do great things in the world. One day soon you will see the amazing woman that I see when I look at you.

To Matt, my wonderful husband, thank you for supporting and loving me, even when you think I have lost my mind. I am so grateful that you came into my life and changed it forever. I love you more than words can say.

To my Lauren, thank you for choosing me to be your mum. You have taught me so much in your lifetime and I am so excited to watch you grow into an incredible woman. You inspire me each and every day.

To everyone who has picked this book up and taken the time to read it, thank you. The only thing I hope for is that it sparks something inside you. My fear is that you will put this book on a shelf and never think again about your dreams. Connect with me on my website or Facebook and keep that dream alive.

www.ingramcontent.com/pod-product-compliance
Lightning Source LLC
Chambersburg PA
CBHW020326010526
44107CB00054B/1995